ON REPENTANCE & DEFEATING DESPAIR

LETTERS TO THEODORE

THE EARLY CHURCH TODAY SERIES

Volume 1

The early leaders of the Church, tasked with shepherding Christ's flock, left us spiritual wealth that is too often neglected in modern times. The Early Church Today Series, published by the St. Mary & St. Moses Abbey Press, aims to help make that richness more accessible to readers, inviting them to see the applicability of the early Church to our walk with God today. By sharing practical selections from the writings of the early Church, aided by meaningful editorial supplements and revisions, each book will attempt to diminish impediments and bring to light what the Church has to offer.

The Early Church Today Series

ST. JOHN CHRYSOSTOM

ON REPENTANCE & DEFEATING DESPAIR

Letters to Theodore

Edited & with an Introduction by

John Habib

ST MARY & MOSES ABBEY PRESS

On Repentance & Defeating Despair: Letters to Theodore
By St. John Chyrosostom

Designed & Published by:
St. Mary & St. Moses Abbey Press
101 S Vista Dr, Sandia, TX 78383
stmabbeypress.com

All Scripture quotations in the footnotes of this book, unless otherwise indicated, are taken from the New King James Version® Copyright © 1982 by Thomas Nelson, Inc. Used by permission. All rights reserved. The rest of the quotations in this book are derived directly from St. John Chrysostom, who is known to have relied on the Septuagint and other early manuscripts available to him.

Library of Congress Control Number: 2018949205

The cover art of this book consists mainly of two ancient images. The arch and design seen at the top of the front and back covers was extracted from a Coptic icon from around the seventh or eighth century portraying St. Mary nursing the infant Christ, which used to be displayed in the formerly inhabited monastery of St. Jeremiah at Saqqara, Egypt (the ancient necropolis of Memphis). The Coptic icon on the front cover is dated to around the thirteenth century, and is from a wall of an ancient church at the Monastery of Saint Anthony in Egypt; it depicts an asectic saint and martyr known as Pakaou grasping a devil named Soufounesar. The intent of choosing this latter image for the cover is to convey the theme and title of this book: defeating despair, which in a sense is defeating the devil who tries to convince us there is no hope for repentance and a life of goodness, and that we should thus remain in despair. By overcoming these thoughts, we overcome the devil who wants us to feel defeated. Instead of feeling overwhelmed by despair, we are empowered by trust in God's forbearance and love, and with this mindset we overwhelm the devil who loses his power over us.

CONTENTS

Second Letter to Theodore

Introduction

ST. JOHN CHRYSOSTOM AND THEODORE

St. John Chrysostom, known as the "golden-mouthed" (designated by the Greek epithet Χρυσόστομος [*Chrysostomos*], anglicized as Chrysostom) due to his eloquent speaking skills and the depth of his uncompromising preaching, was born in the ancient city of Antioch. Shortly after his birth his father died, leaving his mother Anthusa to raise St. John on her own. Elsewhere in Antioch, around the same time, another boy named Theodore was born.

The cultural climate in Antioch that these boys were raised in was full of common worldly pursuits and pleasures of the time: public baths, gaming, and theater to name a few. As one historian put it, "The citizens of Antioch had a reputation for pleasure-seeking, worldliness, fickleness, and cynicism."[1] Almost as if in reaction to such an environment, the outskirts of the city became populated by Christian hermits and monks seeking to escape the vanities of the world.

As Theodore and St. John lived their separate lives, navigating the worldly turbulence around them, their paths eventually converged as they, along with another young

1   J. N. D. Kelly, *Golden Mouth: The Story of John Chrysostom—Ascetic, Preacher, Bishop* (Ithaca, NY: Cornell University Press, 1995), 1–2.

man named Basil, found themselves at the same school around their late teenage years, concluding their education by learning from a well known professor of philosophy, an orator and rhetorician named Libanius. A pagan who detested Christianity, Libanius equipped St. John with skills that ironically contributed to his success as the Christian bishop he eventually came to be. Interestingly, when Libanius was on his deathbed being asked by his friends about who he thought was most worthy to succeed him, he said: "It would have been John, if the Christians had not stolen him from us." The love of Christ truly did dwell in St. John's heart, so much so that after graduating from Libanius's school, St. John became deeply focused on studying Scripture, and eventually joined his childhood friend Basil (who later became a bishop [not to be confused with St. Basil the Great, the bishop of Caesarea]) in living a life of monastic asceticism—the "true philosophy" as St. John called it. Soon afterward, Theodore became a member of this little ascetic brotherhood as well.

It is at this point in the story that we begin to understand the context of the letters St. John wrote to his friend Theodore. As St. John and Basil flourished in their devotion to monastic life, Theodore was enticed and drawn away by his desire for worldly pleasures and fell into worldly habits, among which included being intoxicated by the beauty of a young lady named Hermione, whom he was anxious to marry. Theodore's friends, not the least of whom was St. John Chrysostom, were overcome with sorrow and grief over Theodore's abandonment of his monastic commitment to Christ. Overwhelmed with a desire that his friend Theodore reawaken spiritually, St. John wrote him two letters focused predominantly on convincing him not to fall in despair and to recognize that there is always a path of return to God, no matter how far one has fallen. Many tried to dissuade St. John from his attempts, trying to convince him that seeking Theodore's return was futile and senseless, that he was a "lost cause." However, by God's grace, and through prayers and the appeal of St. John and others, Theodore was moved to return to the true Bridegroom, once more renouncing the world and his matrimonial intentions, and rejoined the monastic brotherhood he had abandoned. Eventually this same Theodore was chosen to become a bishop. These events during the early moments of St. John Chrysostom's life exemplify his pastoral inclinations which, along with his oratory prowess and profound spirituality, contributed to his success and posthumous legacy as the world renown and celebrated archbishop of the great city of Constantinople, commemorated today as a saint in the Church.

References:

J. N. D. Kelly, *Golden Mouth: The Story of John Chrysostom—Ascetic, Preacher, Bishop* (Ithaca, NY: Cornell University Press, 1995).

W. R. W. Stephens, *Introduction to the Letters to Theodore*. In *Nicene and Post-Nicene Fathers: Second Series* 9, Philip Schaff, ed. (1886–1889; repr. New York, NY: Cosimo, Inc., 2007), 87.

Introduction to the Treatise on the Priesthood, ibid., 27–29.

EDITORIAL REMARKS: HOW THESE LETTERS ARE PRESENTED IN THIS BOOK

The purpose of this book is to make St. John's letters to Theodore more accessible to modern audiences. Several editorial supplements and revisions were implemented to help achieve that end:

1. The text of this book was derived from the translation overseen by Philip Schaff in the *Nicene and Post-Nicene Fathers* (NPNF),[2] and was further revised as minimally as possible to replace archaic words with modern equivalents, and to implement syntactic improvements. (Note: St. John Chrysostom's quotes from Scripture, having been derived from the Septuagint and early biblical manuscripts, were kept mostly intact in order to preserve their meaning and structure as St. John would have known them. Accordingly, some verses may be slightly varied from modern Bible translations and versions.)

2. Recognizing that many are dissuaded from offering a diligent attempt to read the writings of the Church Fathers, it was our hope to alleviate some of the reasons we anticipate cause this, which we surmised as consisting of two main points: the Church Father texts available often appear to require too much reading, and the texts themselves seem too difficult to understand. We tried addressing both issues as follows, which are additions by the editor and not part of St. John's original work:

2 *Nicene and Post-Nicene Fathers: Second Series* 9, Philip Schaff, ed. (1886–1889; repr. New York, NY: Cosimo, Inc., 2007).

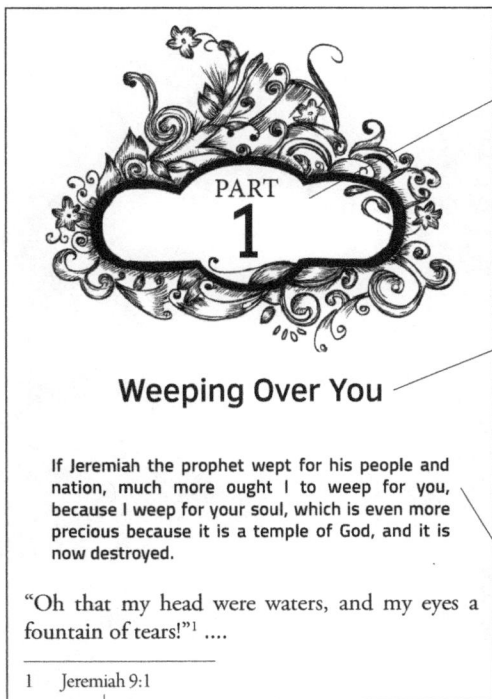

PART 1

We adopted the partitioning of the NPNF text and treated them each like chapters, making them short, consumable segments.

Weeping Over You

For each part, we added in a title, to help the reader understand the prominent or notable theme that they can expect from the text they are about to read.

If Jeremiah the prophet wept for his people and nation, much more ought I to weep for you, because I weep for your soul, which is even more precious because it is a temple of God, and it is now destroyed.

"Oh that my head were waters, and my eyes a fountain of tears!"[1] ....

_____
1   Jeremiah 9:1

Verse references as we know them today did not exist during St. John's time. Footnotes in this text will provide modern-day verse references, as well as other editorial notes.

The text was further segmented and prefaced by summarized paraphrases as an aid for the reader to comprehend what they are about to read. These summaries are meant to take what St. John Chrysostom wrote, and recast it in a simpler, concise, contemporary manner of writing. While they can be read on their own, they certainly are not intended to displace the beauty of St. John Chrysostom's words, but rather are provided as a guide so that the reader is aided in understanding the more lofty and eloquent text they are about to delve into. Moreover, this should also help in navigating through the book and returning to specific segments of St. John's letters.

St. John Chrysostom's

FIRST LETTER TO THEODORE

Weeping Over You

If Jeremiah the prophet wept for his people and nation, much more ought I to weep for you, because I weep for your soul, which is even more precious because it is a temple of God, and it is now destroyed.

"Oh that my head were waters, and my eyes a fountain of tears!"[1] It is timely for me to utter these words now, yes much more than for the prophet in his time. For although I am not about to mourn over many cities, or whole nations, yet I shall mourn over a soul which is of equal value with many such nations, yes even more precious. For if one man who does the will of God is better than ten thousand transgressors, then you were formerly better than

---

1   Jeremiah 9:1

ten thousand Jews.[2] Therefore no one would now blame me if I were to compose more lamentations than those which are contained in the prophet [Jeremiah's writings], and to utter complaints yet more vehement.

For it is not the overthrow of a city which I mourn, nor the captivity of wicked then, but the desolation of a sacred soul, the destruction and effacement of a Christ-bearing temple.[3] For would not anyone groan, imitating the lamentation of the prophet, who knew in the days of its glory that well-ordered mind of yours, which the devil has now set on fire; when he hears that barbarian hands have defiled the holy of holies, and have set fire to all things and burned them up, the cherubim, the ark, the mercy seat, the tablets of stone, the golden pot? For this calamity is more bitter, yes more bitter than that, in proportion as the pledges deposited in your soul were far more precious than those. This temple is holier than that; for it glistened not with gold and silver, but with the grace of the Spirit, and in place of the ark and the cherubim, it had Christ, and His Father, and the Paraclete seated within. But now

---

2   Jeremiah, who St. John Chrysostom just referred to, was deeply troubled and wept for the poor spiritual condition of the Jews at his time, who had forsaken God in a multitude of ways. St. John is saying here, if one righteous person is more revered by God than ten thousand people who forsake Him, then when Theodore was living a righteous life, he was more precious than the multitude of Jews that Jeremiah was weeping about who transgressed God's commandments.

3   "Do you not know that you are the temple of God and that the Spirit of God dwells in you? If anyone defiles the temple of God, God will destroy him. For the temple of God is holy, which temple you are" (1 Corinthians 3:16–17); "Or do you not know that your body is the temple of the Holy Spirit who is in you, whom you have from God, and you are not your own?" (1 Corinthians 6:19).

all is changed, and the temple is desolate, and bare of its former beauty and comeliness, unadorned with its divine and unspeakable adornments, destitute of all security and protection; it has neither door nor bolt, and is laid open to all manner of soul-destroying and shameful thoughts; and if the thought of arrogance or fornication, or greed, or any more accursed than these, wish to enter in, there is no one to hinder them; whereas formerly, even as heaven is inaccessible to all these, so also was the purity of your soul.

> **People may find it strange that I weep over your condition, but I will not stop until you change, because with God all things are possible. Do not fall in despair; if the devil brought you down, God is more capable of raising you up. You just need to look to God for pity and mercy, and persevere.**

Now perhaps I shall seem to say what is incredible to some who now witness your desolation and overthrow; for on this account I wail and mourn, and shall not cease doing so, until I see you again established in your former luster. For although this seems to be impossible to men, yet to God all things are possible. For it is He "who raises the poor from the earth, and lifts up the beggar from the dunghill, to set him with the princes, even with the princes of his people."[4] It is He "who makes the barren woman to dwell at home, a mother rejoicing over her children."[5]

---

4   Psalm 113:7, 8

5   Psalm 113:9

Do not then despair of the most perfect change. For if the devil had such great power as to cast you down from that pinnacle and height of virtue into the extremity of evil doing, much more will God be able to draw you up again to your former confidence; and not only indeed to make you what you were before, but even much happier. Only do not be downcast, nor fling away good hopes, nor fall into the condition of the ungodly. For it is not the multitude of sins which is apt to plunge men into despair, but impiety of soul. Therefore Solomon did not make the unqualified statement, "Every one who has entered into the den of the wicked, despises," but only "he who is ungodly."[6] For it is such persons only who are affected in this way when they have entered the den of the wicked. And this it is which does not permit them to look up, and re-ascend to the position from which they fell. For this accursed thought pressing down like some yoke upon the neck of the soul, and so forcing it to stoop, hinders it from looking up to the Master. Now it is the part of a brave and excellent man to break this yoke in pieces, to shake off the tormentor fastened upon him, and to utter the words of the prophet: "As the eyes of a maiden look unto the hands of her mistress, even so our eyes look unto the Lord our God until He has mercy upon us. Have pity upon us, O Lord, have pity upon us, for we have been utterly

---

6   Proverbs 18:3, according to the Septuagint. A better reading of this may be: "When an ungodly man comes into a depth of evils, he despises them; but dishonor and reproach come upon him." St. John seems to be conveying this verse as saying that when one is truly ungodly, then when they find themselves ensnared by sin will they feel worthless about themselves; but the right-minded who have hope in God do not fall into the feeling of despising oneself, despite their sins.

filled with contempt."[7] Truly divine are these precepts and decrees of the highest form of spiritual wisdom. We have been filled, it is said, with contempt, and have undergone countless distresses; nevertheless we shall not desist from looking up to God, neither shall we cease praying to Him until He has received our petition. For this is the mark of a noble soul, not to be cast down, nor be dismayed at the multitude of the calamities which oppress it, nor to withdraw, after praying many times without success, but to persevere, until He has mercy upon us, even as the blessed David says.

---

7   Psalm 123:2, 3

The Devil Wants You to Lose Hope

The devil strives to bring us into despair by cutting off our hope in God, which keeps us connected to heaven.

For the reason why the devil plunges us into thoughts of despair is that he may cut off the hope which is towards God, the safe anchor, the foundation of our life, the guide of the way which leads to heaven, the salvation of perishing souls. "For by hope" it is said, "we are saved."[1] For this assuredly it is which, like some strong cord suspended from the heavens, supports our souls, gradually drawing towards that world on high those who cling firmly to it, and lifting them above the tempest of the evils of this life. If anyone then becomes enervated, and lets go of this

---

1   Romans 8:24

sacred anchor, straightway he falls down, and is suffocated, having entered into the abyss of wickedness. And the evil one knowing this, when he perceives that we are ourselves oppressed by the consciousness of evil deeds, steps in himself and lays upon us the additional burden, heavier than lead, of anxiety arising from despair; and if we accept it, it follows of necessity that we are immediately dragged down by the weight, and having been parted from that cord, descend into the depth of misery where you yourself are now, having forsaken the commandments of the meek and lowly Master, and executing all the injunctions of the cruel tyrant and implacable enemy of our salvation; having broken in pieces the easy yoke, and cast away the light burden, and having put on the iron collar instead of these things; yes, having hung the ponderous millstone[2] from your neck. Where then can you find a footing hereafter when you are submerging your unhappy soul, imposing on yourself this necessity of continually sinking downwards?

Mourn with me, because I've lost someone so precious.

Now the woman who had found the one coin called her neighbors to share her joy, saying, "Rejoice with me";[3] but I shall now invoke all friends, both mine and yours, for the

---

2   The millstone referred to here is one that is moved by a donkey, and is therefore much heavier and even more cumbersome to use than the common hand-mill. This type of millstone was also mentioned in Matthew 18:6.

3   Luke 15:9

contrary purpose, not to say "rejoice with me," but "mourn with me," and take up the same strain of mourning, and utter the same cry of distress with me. For the worst possible loss has befallen me, not that some given number of talents of gold or some large quantity of precious stones have dropped out of my hand, but that he who was more precious than all these things, who was sailing over this same sea, this great and broad sea with me, has, I know not how, slipped overboard, and fallen into the very pit of destruction.

Keep Fighting

While it is not godly and wise to mourn over people who have died physically, on the other hand it is definitely justified and godly to mourn over a soul that has lost its way, for which one should mourn until the person returns to God.

Now if any should attempt to divert me from mourning, I shall reply to them in the words of the prophet, saying, "Let me alone, I will weep bitterly; do not labor to comfort me."[1] For the mourning with which I mourn now is not of a kind to subject me to condemnation for excess in lamentation, but the cause is one for which even Paul, or Peter, had they been here, would not have been ashamed

---

1   Isaiah 22:4

to weep and mourn, and reject all kinds of consolation. For those who bewail that death which is common to all, one might reasonably accuse them of much feebleness of spirit; but when in place of a corpse a dead soul lies before us, pierced with innumerable wounds, and yet even in its death manifesting its former natural comeliness, and health, and beauty now extinguished, who can be so harsh and unsympathetic as to utter words of encouragement in place of wailing and lamentation? For as in the other world the absence of mourning is a mark of divine wisdom, so in this world the act of mourning is a mark of the same. He who had already made his way up to the sky, who was laughing to scorn the vanity of this life, who regarded bodily beauty no more than if it had been in forms of stone, who despised gold as if it had been mud, and every kind of luxury as mire, even he, having been suddenly overwhelmed with the feverish longing of a preposterous passion, has ruined his health, and manly strength, and the bloom of his youth, and become a slave of pleasure. Shall we not weep then, I pray you, for such a man and bewail him, until we have got him back again?

It is senseless to lament over someone who died and cannot return, yet sensible to mourn over a soul that may be able to return to God.

And where do these things concern the human soul? It is not possible indeed to discover in this world the means of release from the death of the body, and yet even this does not stop the mourners from lamenting; but only in this world is it possible to render ineffective the death of the soul. "For in Hades" we read, "who will confess you?" Is it not then the height of stupidity that they who mourn the death of the body should do this so earnestly, although they know that they will not raise the dead man to life by their lamentation, but that we should not manifest anything of the kind, and this when we know that often there is hope of conducting the lost soul back to its former life?

> Many at present and in the past fell in sin and were able to come out of it and be numbered among the saints. Continue progressing and you'll find a refreshing path ahead.

For many both now and in the days of our forefathers, having been perverted from the right position, and fallen headlong out of the straight path, have been so completely restored as to eclipse their former deeds by the latter, and to receive the prize, and be wreathed with the garland of victory, and be proclaimed among the conquerors, and be numbered in the company of the saints. For as long as anyone stands in the furnace of pleasures, even if he has countless examples of this kind before him, the thing seems to him to be impossible; but if he once gets a short start upon the way out from there, by continually advancing he leaves the fiercer part of the fire behind him and will see the parts which are in front of him, and before his footsteps [the way will be] full of dew and much refreshment.

> **Falling into despair keeps us from fighting and competing in the race, which is what the devil wants; instead we need to keep struggling and fighting no matter how many times we fall.**

Only let us not despair or grow weary of the return; for he who is so affected, even if he has acquired boundless power and zeal, has acquired it to no purpose. For when he has once shut the door of repentance against himself, and has blocked the entrance into the racecourse, how will he be able while he abides outside to accomplish any good thing, either small or great? On this account the evil one uses all kinds of devices in order to plant in us this thought (of despair); for (if he succeeds) he will no longer have to sweat and toil in contending with us; how should he, when we are prostrate and fallen, and unwilling to resist him? For he who has been able to slip out of this chain will recover his own strength and will not cease struggling against the devil to his last gasp; and even if he had countless other falls, he will get up again, and will smite his enemy; but he who is in bondage to the cogitations of despair, and has unstrung his own strength, how will he be able to prevail, and to resist, having on the contrary taken to flight?

God Disciplines Out of Love

Even if a person, a Christian, has fallen into the worst of sins for an extended time, even unto old age, such a person should not fall into despair; they should know that God's punishments are out of His care for them.

And speak not to me of those who have committed small sins, but suppose the case of one who is filled full of all wickedness, and let him practice everything which excludes him from the kingdom; and let us suppose that this man is not one of those who were unbelievers from the beginning, but formerly belonged to the believers, and such as were well pleasing to God, but afterwards has become a fornicator, adulterer, effeminate, a thief, a drunkard, a sodomite, a reviler, and everything else of this kind; I will not approve even of this man despairing of himself, although he may have gone on to extreme old age in the practice of this great and unspeakable wickedness. For if the wrath of God were a passion, one might well despair as being unable to quench the flame which he had kindled by so many evil doings; but since the divine nature is passionless, even if He punishes, even if He takes vengeance, He does this not with wrath, but with tender care, and much loving-kindness; wherefore it behooves us to be of much good courage, and to trust in the power of repentance.

> **God punishes, not because you've injured Him (because sin only truly injured you), but so He can attract you to Him again.**

For even those who have sinned against Him He is not in the habit of visiting with punishment for His own sake; for no harm can traverse that divine nature; but He acts with a view to our advantage, and to prevent our perverseness becoming worse by our making a practice of despising and neglecting Him. For even as one who places himself outside the light inflicts no loss on the light, but the greatest upon himself being shut up in darkness, even so he who has become accustomed to despise that almighty power, does no injury to the power, but inflicts the greatest possible injury upon himself. And for this reason God threatens us with punishments, and often inflicts them, not as avenging Himself, but by way of attracting us to Himself. For a physician also is not distressed or vexed at the insults of those who are out of their minds, but yet does and contrives everything for the purpose of stopping those who do such unseemly acts, not looking to his own interests but to their profit; and if they manifest some small degree of self-control and sobriety he rejoices and is glad, and applies his remedies much more earnestly, not as revenging himself upon them for their former conduct, but as wishing to increase their advantage, and to bring them back to a purely sound state of health. Even so God, when we fall into the very extremity of madness, says and does everything, not by way of avenging Himself on account of our former deeds, but because He wishes to release us from our disorder; and by means of right reason it is quite possible to be convinced of this.

Despair Is Not Justifiable

If anyone thinks someone is justified to fall in despair due to repeated sins for an extended time, take the example of King Nebuchadnezzar, who after repeated transgressions following so many wondrous events and miracles, God kept giving him a chance to repent until he eventually did.

Now if anyone should dispute with us concerning these things, we will confirm them out of the divine oracles. For who, I ask, became more depraved than the king of the Babylonians, who after having received such a great experience of God's power as to make obeisance to His prophet, and commanded offerings and incense to be sacrificed to Him,[1] was again carried away to his former

---

1   Daniel 2:46

pride, and cast bound into the furnace those who did
not honor himself before God.[2] Nevertheless this man
who was so cruel and impious, and a beast rather than
a human being, God invited to repentance, and granted
him several opportunities of conversion: first of all the
miracle which took place in the furnace, and after that the
vision which the king saw but which Daniel interpreted,
a vision sufficient to bend even a heart of stone; and in
addition to these things, after the exhortation derived
from [these] events, the prophet also himself advised him
saying, "Therefore, O king, let my counsel please you, and
redeem your sins by alms, and your iniquities by showing
mercy to the poor; it may be that long-suffering will be
shown to your offense."[3]

What say you O wise and blessed man? After so great
a fall is there again a way of return? And after so great
a disease is health possible? And after so great a madness
is there again a hope of soundness of mind? The king
had deprived himself beforehand of all hope, first of all
by having ignored Him who created him and conducted
him to this honor, although he had many evidences of His
power and forethought to recount [that] which occurred
both in his own case and in the case of his forefathers. But
after this again, when he had received distinct tokens of
God's wisdom and foreknowledge, and had seen magic,
and astronomy, and the theater of the whole satanic
system of jugglery overthrown, he exhibited deeds yet
worse than the former. For things which the wise magi,

2   Daniel 3
3   Daniel 4:27

the Gazarenes,[4] could not explain, but confessed that they were beyond human nature, these a captive youth having caused to be solved for him, so moved him by that miracle that he not only himself believed, but also became to the whole world a clear herald and teacher of this doctrine.[5] Wherefore if even before having received such a token it was unpardonable in him to ignore God, much more so was it after that miracle, and his confession, and the teaching which was extended to others. For if he had not honestly believed that He was the only true God, he would not have shown such honor to His servant, or have laid down such laws for others. But yet after making this kind of confession, he again lapsed into idolatry, and he who once fell on his face and made obeisance to the servant of God broke out into such a pitch of madness as to cast into the furnace the servants of God who did not make obeisance to himself.

What then? Did God visit the apostate, as he deserved to be visited? No! He supplied him with greater tokens of His own power, drawing him back again after so great a display of arrogance to his former condition. And, what is yet more wonderful, that owing to the abundance of

---

4   Modern bible translations, such as the NKJV, use the word "soothsayers" (see Daniel 5:7, 11, 15). However, the Septuagint, the Greek translation of the Old Testament used by the apostles, as well as the early fathers such as St. John Chrysostom, leaves the word untranslated, and so renders it as Gazarenes. Some understood it as referring to a people or nation, while others understood the word to refer to a certain group of people who purportedly could foresee the future, as the modern translations imply (the Hebrew word can mean "to determine," implying the meaning here of one who "determines the future").

5   Daniel 2

the miracles he might not again disbelieve what was done, the subject upon which He wrought the sign was none other than the furnace which the king himself kindled for the children whom he bound and cast therein. Even to extinguish the flame would have been a wonderful and strange thing, but the benign Deity, in order to inspire him with greater fear, and increase his dismay, and undo all his hardness of heart, did what was greater and stranger than this. For, permitting the furnace to be kindled to as high a pitch as he desired, He then exhibited His own peculiar power, not by putting down the devices of His enemies, but by frustrating them when they were set on foot. And, to prevent anyone who saw them survive the flame from supposing that it was a vision, He permitted those who cast them in to be burned, thus proving that the thing seen was really fire; for otherwise it would not have devoured naphtha and tow, and fagots[6] and such a large number of bodies; but nothing is stronger than His

6   This is derived from an excerpt in the book of Daniel that is canonical according to the Orthodox Church and was included in the Greek translation of the Old Testament (the Septuagint) used by the apostles and early Fathers, but was later excluded by some denominations and therefore considered apocryphal by them. The excerpt that mentions these three words here—naphtha, tow, and fagots—extends the story of the three youth in the fiery furnace in the Book of Daniel, and includes the praise chanted by them while present amid the fire. While the words may seem foreign to the modern reader, here is what they are thought to mean: naphtha, also known as rosin or pitch, is understood as being a substance from the resin of plants that is highly flammable; tow appears to be a sort of short thread from a type of flax plant, which is also highly flammable; and fagot seems to refer to a bundle of sticks that would be burned. What is meant by their use here is that the fire that the three youth were thrown into was not an imaginary vision, but real fire that burns, as Scripture indicates these flammable substances were among those things which actually burned.

command; but the nature of all existing things obeys Him who brought them into being out of nothing, which was just what He manifested at that time, for the flame having received perishable bodies, held aloof from them as if they had been imperishable, and restored in safety, with the addition of much luster, the deposit entrusted to it. For like kings from some royal court, even so did those children come forth from the furnace, no one having the patience to look any longer at the king, but all transferring their eyes from him to the strange spectacle, and neither the diadem nor the purple robe, nor any other feature of royal pomp, attracted the multitudes of unbelievers so much as the sight of those faithful ones, who tarried long in the fire, and then came out of it as men might have done who had undergone this in a dream. For the most fragile of all our features, I mean the hair, prevailed more mightily than adamant against the all-devouring flame. And the fact that when they were cast into the midst of the fire they suffered no harm was not the only wonder, but the further fact that they were speaking the whole time. Now all who have witnessed persons burning are aware that if they keep their lips fast closed, they can hold out for a short time at least against the conflagration; but if anyone chances to open his mouth, the soul instantly takes its flight from the body.

Nevertheless after such great miracles had taken place, and all who were present and beheld were amazed, and those who were absent had been informed of the fact by means of letters, the king who instructed others remained himself without correction, and went back again to his former wickedness. And yet even then God did not punish him, but was still long-suffering, counseling him both by means of visions and by His prophet. But when he was not made at all better by any of these things, then at last God inflicted punishment upon him, not by way of avenging Himself on account of his former deeds, but as cutting off the occasion of future evils, and checking the advance of wickedness, and He did not inflict even this permanently, but after having chastised him for a few years, He restored him again to his former honor, without having suffered any loss from his punishment, but on the contrary having gained the greatest possible good—a firm hold upon faith in God, and repentance on account of his former misdeeds.[7]

---

7   Daniel 4

God's Mercy Is Boundless

God accepts even the slightest bit of repentance, even if not "complete," as He did with many in the past who relied on the boundlessness of God's mercy rather than the magnitude of their iniquities.

For such is the loving-kindness of God: He never turns His face away from a sincere repentance, but if anyone has pushed on to the very extremity of wickedness, and chooses to return from there towards the path of virtue, God accepts and welcomes, and does everything so as to restore him to his former position.

And He does what is yet more merciful, for even should anyone not manifest complete repentance, He does not pass by one which is small and insignificant, but assigns a great reward even to this, which is evident from what Isaiah the prophet says concerning the people of the Jews, speaking in this manner: "On account of his sin I put him to pain for a little while, and smote him, and turned My face away from him, and he was pained, and walked sorrowfully, and then I healed him, and comforted him."[1] And we might cite as another witness that most ungodly king who was given over to sin by the influence of his wife; yet when he only sorrowed, and put on sackcloth, and condemned his offenses, he so won for himself the mercy of God as to be released from all the evils which were impending over him. For God said to Elijah: "See how Ahab is pricked in the heart before My face? I will not bring the evil upon him in his own days, because he has wept before Me."[2] And after this again, Manasseh, having exceeded all in fury and tyranny, and having subverted the legal form of worship, and shut up the temple, and caused the deceit of idolatry to flourish, and having become more ungodly than all who were before him, when he afterwards repented, was ranked among the friends of God. Now, if looking to the magnitude of his own iniquities he had despaired of restoration and repentance, he would have missed all which he afterwards obtained; but as it was, looking to the boundlessness of God's tender mercy instead of the enormity of his transgressions, and having broken apart the bonds of the devil, he rose up and contended with him, and finished the good course.[3]

---

1   Isaiah 57:17, 18

2   1 Kings 21:29

3   2 Chronicles 33:10–19

Repentance is not judged or rewarded by the quantity of time you spend offering it, but by how genuine it is when it is offered.

And not only by what was done to these men, but also by the words of the prophet does God destroy the counsels of despair, speaking in this manner: "Today, if you will hear His voice, harden not your hearts, as in the provocation."[4] Now that expression "today" may be uttered at every time of life, even on the verge of old age, if you desire it, for repentance is judged not by the quantity of time, but by the disposition of the soul. For the Ninevites did not need many days to blot out their sin, but the short space of one day availed to efface all their iniquity;[5] and the robber also did not take a long time to effect his entrance into Paradise, but in such a brief moment as one might occupy in uttering a single word did he wash off all the sins which he had committed in his whole life, and received the prize bestowed by the divine approval even before the apostles.[6] And we also see the martyrs obtain glorious crowns for themselves in the course, not of many years, but of a few days, and often in a single day only.

---

4 Psalm 95:7–8: provocation refers to the time when the people of Israel rebelled against God as they wandered in the wilderness for forty years.

5 Jonah 3–4

6 Luke 23:32–43

It's Not About Falling
It's About Getting Up

To have fallen is not a grievous thing, but rather to remain prostrate after falling, and not to get up again, continuing in despair. Many examples exist of how those who were believers fell and returned.

Wherefore we have need of zeal in every direction, and much preparation of mind; and if we so order our conscience as to hate our former wickedness, and choose the contrary path with as much energy as God desires and commands, we shall not have anything less on account of the short space of time.[1] Many at least who were last have

---

1   In accordance with his previous remarks, St. John is saying, "Just because we do not spend an extended amount of time offering a life of repentance does not diminish the extent to which the repentance is accepted."

far outstripped those who were first. For to have fallen is not a grievous thing, but to remain prostrate after falling, and not to get up again, and, playing the coward and the sluggard, to conceal feebleness of moral purpose under the reasoning of despair, to whom also the prophet spoke in perplexity saying: "Does he who fall not rise up, or he who turns away not turn back?"[2]

But if you inquire of me for instances of persons who have fallen away after having believed, all these things have been said with reference to such persons, for he who has fallen belonged formerly to those who were standing, not to those who were prostrate; for how should one in that condition fall? But other things also shall be said, partly by means of parables, partly by plainer deeds and words.

Now that sheep which was separated from the ninety-nine,[3] and then was brought back again, represents to us nothing else than the fall and return of the faithful; for it was a sheep not of some alien flock, but belonging to the same number as the rest, and was formerly pastured by the same shepherd. And it strayed on no common straying, but wandered away to the mountains and in valleys—that is to say, some long journey, distant from the right path. Did he then allow it to stray? By no means, but brought it back neither driving it, nor beating it, but taking it upon his shoulders. For as the best physicians bring back those who are far gone in sickness with careful treatment to a state of health, not only treating them according to the

---

2   Jeremiah 8:4

3   Luke 15:4–5

laws of the medical art, but sometimes also giving them gratification, even so God conducts to virtue those who are much depraved, not with great severity, but gently and gradually, and supporting them on every side, so that the separation may not become greater, nor the error more prolonged.

And the same truth is implied in the parable of the prodigal son as well as in this. For he also was no stranger, but a son, and a brother of the child who had been well pleasing to the father; and he plunged into no ordinary vice, but went to the very extremity, so to say, of evil, he the rich and free and well-bred son being reduced to a more miserable condition than that of household slaves, strangers, and hirelings. Nevertheless he returned again to his original condition, and had his former honor restored to him. But if he had despaired of his life, and, dejected by what had befallen him, had remained in the foreign land, he would not have obtained what he did obtain, but would have been consumed with hunger, and so have undergone the most pitiable death. But since he repented, and did not despair, he was restored, even after such great corruption, to the same splendor as before, and was arrayed in the most beautiful robe, and enjoyed greater honors than his brother who had not fallen. For "these many years," he says, "do I serve you, neither have I transgressed your commandment at any time, and yet you never gave me a young goat, that I might make merry with my friends; but when this your son has come who has devoured your living with harlots, you have killed for him the fatted calf."[4] So

---

4   Luke 15:29–30

great is the power of repentance.

God Always Seeks Your Return

Do not despair due to a feeling that you cannot be reconciled to God, because nothing prevents your reconciliation to Him.

Having then such great examples, let us not continue in evil, nor despair of reconciliation, but let us say also ourselves, "I will go to my Father," and let us draw near to God. For He Himself never turns away from us, but it is we who put ourselves far off:[1] for "I am a God," we read,

---

1   This is reminiscent of a contemplation by the late pope of Alexandria, His Holiness Pope Shenouda III, which he once shared: we tend to say the "sun goes down," as if it is leaving us, but on the contrary, it is the the earth which rotates and turns away from view of the sun. So too, we may think God has turned away from us, when in fact it is us who have turned away from Him.

"at hand and not a God afar off."[2] And again, when He was rebuking them by the mouth of this prophet He said: "Do not your sins separate between you and Me."[3] Inasmuch then as this is the cause which puts us far from God, let us remove this obnoxious barrier, which prevents any near approach being made.

> Take the example of the Corinthian who strayed afar off and was called back, as well as the Galatians who were deemed to have "fallen from grace," showing that after extreme perversion it is possible for Christ to be formed again in us, for that is His Desire, not our death.

But now hear how this has actually occurred in real instances. Among the Corinthians some eminent man committed a sin such as was not named even among the Gentiles. This man was a believer and belonged to the household of Christ; and some say that he was actually a member of the priesthood. What then? Did Paul cut him off from the communion of those who were in the way of salvation. By no means, for he himself it is who rebukes the Corinthians countless times, backwards and forwards, because they did not bring the man to a state of repentance. However, desiring to prove to us that there is no sin which cannot be healed, he said again concerning

---

2   Jeremiah 22:23

3   Isaiah 59:2. It appears St. John meant to refer to Isaiah rather than Jeremiah. Alternatively, he may have intended Jeremiah 5:25: "Your iniquities have turned these things away, and your sins have withheld good from you."

the man who had transgressed more grievously than the Gentiles: "Deliver such a one to Satan for destruction of the flesh, that his spirit may be saved in the day of the Lord Jesus Christ."[4] Now this was prior to repentance, but after he had repented, "Sufficient," said he, "for such a one is this punishment which was inflicted by the many"; and he charged them by a letter to console the man again, and to welcome his repentance, so that he should not be overcome by Satan.

Moreover, when the whole Galatian people fell after having believed, and wrought miracles, and endured many trials for the sake of their faith in Christ, he sets them up again. For that they had done miracles he testified when he said: "He therefore that supplies to you the Spirit and works miracles among you."[5] And that they endured many contests for the sake of the faith, he also testified when he says: "Have you suffered so many things in vain if it be indeed in vain?"[6] Nevertheless after making so great an advance they committed sin sufficient to estrange them from Christ, concerning which he declares saying: "Behold, I Paul tell you, that if you become circumcised, Christ will profit you nothing";[7] and again "you who would be justified by the law are fallen away from grace."[8] And yet even after so great a lapse he welcomes them saying, "My little children, for whom I am in travail again until Christ

---

4   1 Corinthians 5:5

5   Galatians 3:5

6   Galatians 3:4

7   Galatians 5:2

8   Galatians 5:4

is formed in you," showing that after extreme perversion it is possible for Christ to be formed again in us, for He does not desire the death of a sinner, but rather that he should be brought back and live.[9]

---

9   Ezekiel 18:23, 32

Even the Slightest Bit of Repentance Counts

Let us seek God, for He prepared heaven for us, as opposed to hell which was prepared for the devil.

Let us then turn to Him, my beloved friend, and carry out the will of God. For He created us and brought us into being, that He might make us partakers of eternal blessings, that He might offer us the kingdom of heaven, not that He might cast us into hell and deliver us to the fire; for this was made not for us, but for the devil, but for us the kingdom has been destined and made ready long ago. And by way of indicating both these truths He says to those on the right hand, "Come you blessed of My Father, inherit the kingdom prepared for you from the foundation of the world";[1] but to those on the left, "Depart from Me, you cursed, into fire everlasting prepared"—He no longer says "for you" but—"for the devil and his angels."[2] Thus hell has not been made for us but for him and his angels: but the kingdom has been prepared for us before the foundation of the world.

Repent when it counts, during this life, because after we die not even the most earnest of repentance will be of any profit.

Let us not then make ourselves unworthy of entrance into the bride-chamber, for as long as we are in this world, even if we commit countless sins it is possible to wash them all away by manifesting repentance for our offenses; but when once we have departed to the other world, even if we display the most earnest repentance it will be of no benefit, not even if we gnash our teeth, beat our breasts, and utter innumerable calls for relief, no one with the tip of his finger will apply a drop to our burning bodies, but we shall only hear those words which the rich man heard in the parable: "Between us and you a great gulf has been fixed."[3] Let us then, I beseech you, recover our senses here and let us recognize our Master as He ought to be recognized, for

---

1   Matthew 25:34

2   Matthew 25:41

3   Luke 16:26

only when we are in Hades should we abandon the hope derived from repentance, because there only is this remedy weak and unprofitable. But while we are here, even if it is applied in old age itself, it exhibits much strength.

> **The devil knows that God counts even the smallest bit of repentance, just as God takes into account the smallest of sins.**

Wherefore also the devil sets everything in motion in order to root in us the reasoning which comes of despair, for he knows that if we repent even a little we shall not do this without some reward. But just as he who gives a cup of cold water has his recompense reserved for him,[4] so also the man who has repented of the evils which he has done, even if he cannot exhibit the repentance which his offenses deserve, will have a commensurate reward. For not a single item of good, however small it may be, will be overlooked by the righteous Judge. For if He makes such an exact scrutiny of our sins, as to require punishment for both our words and thoughts, much more will our good deeds, whether they be great or small, be reckoned to our credit at that day.

> **Just because you cannot immediately return to your former spiritual stature, do not waste more time waiting**

---

4   Matthew 10:42

to repent. Before you repent, the road ahead seems so difficult, which is what Satan wants you to think, but after repentance you will realize the path is not as distressing as you thought.

Therefore, even if you are not able to return again to the most exact state of discipline, yet if you withdraw yourself in a slight degree at least from your present disorder and excess, even this will not be impossible; only set yourself to the task at once, and open the entrance into the place of contest. But as long as you tarry outside, this naturally seems difficult and impracticable to you. For before making the trial, even if things are easy and manageable, they are accustomed to present an appearance of much difficulty to us; but when we are actually engaged in the trial, and making the venture, the greater part of our distress is removed, and confidence taking the place of tremor and despair lessens the fear and increases the facility of operation, and makes our good hopes stronger. For this reason also the wicked one dragged Judas out of this world lest he should make a fair beginning, and so return by means of repentance to the point from which he fell. For although it may seem a strange thing to say, I will not admit even that sin to be too great for the assistance in time of distress which is brought to us from repentance. Wherefore I pray and beseech you to banish all this satanic mode of thinking from your soul, and to return to this state of salvation. For if indeed I were commanding you to ascend to your former altitude all at once, you would naturally complain of there being much difficulty in doing this; but [what] if all which I now ask you to do is to get up and return to your former state and shrink, and make a backward movement?

Have you noticed what happens to people who live a life of luxury, sin, and indulgence? Their life ends in a coffin with dust and worms. But then think beyond the grave where they are, suffering from the undying worm, unquenchable fire, outer darkness, and other afflictions. If we focus during this life on keeping down the flame of desires, then in the next life we will not have to suffer from the punishment of eternal flames.

Have you not seen those who have died in the midst of luxury and drunkenness, and sport, and all the other folly of this life? Where are they now who used to strut through the marketplace with much pomp, and a crowd of attendants, who were clothed in silk and redolent with perfumes, and kept a table for their musicians, the attentions of flatterers, the loud laughter, the relaxation of spirit, the enervation of mind, the voluptuous, abandoned, extravagant manner of life? It has all come to an end. Where now have all these things taken their flight? What has become of the body which enjoyed so much attention, and cleanliness. Go your way to the coffin, behold the dust, the ashes, the worms, behold the loathsomeness of the place, and groan bitterly. And if only the penalty were limited to the ashes! But now transfer your thought from the coffin and these worms to that undying worm, to the fire unquenchable, to the gnashing of teeth, to the outer darkness, to affliction and distress, to the parable of Lazarus and the rich man, who although the owner of so much wealth, and clothed in purple, could not become the owner of even a drop of water; and this when he was placed in a condition of such great necessity.

The things of this world are in their nature no way better than dreams. For just as those who work in the mines or suffer some other kind of punishment more severe than this, when they have fallen asleep owing to their many weary toils and the extreme bitterness of their life, and in their dreams see themselves living in luxury and prosperity, [they] are in no way grateful to their dreams after they have awoken, even so that rich man having become rich in this present life, as it were in a dream, after his departure consequently was punished with that bitter punishment. Consider these things, and having contrasted that fire with the conflagration of desires which now possesses you, release yourself from the furnace. For he who has thoroughly quenched this furnace here, will have no experience of that in the other world; but if a man does not get the better of this furnace here, the other will lay hold of him more vehemently when he has departed from here.

How long do you expect life to be? No one can guarantee its extent or quality. But temporary pleasures are not worth the eternal consequence. Consider all your deeds within an eternal perspective.

How long a time do you wish the enjoyment of the present life to be extended? For I do not suppose indeed that more than fifty years remain to you so as to reach extreme old age, nor indeed is even this at all assured to us, for how should they who cannot be confident about living even to the evening rely upon so many years as these? And not only is this uncertain, but there is the uncertainty also of a change in our affairs, for often when life has been extended for a long period, the conditions of luxury have not been extended with it, but have come, and at the same time hastily departed. However, if you like, let it be granted for argument's sake that you will live so many years, and will not sustain any reverse of fortune; what is this compared with the endless ages, and those bitter and intolerable punishments? For here indeed both good and evil things have an end, and that very speedily; but there, both are coextensive with immortal ages, and in their quality differ unspeakably from the things which now are.

Pleasures Are Not Worth the Eternal Price

The fire of eternal punishment in the afterlife is unlike fire here in this world—it being unquenchable, giving no light, and imposing suffering and dismay eternally, for the souls of sinners in the afterlife will be immortal and thus continually be subject to such unyielding, chastising punishments.

For when you hear of fire, do not suppose the fire in that world to be like this, for fire in this world burns up and makes away with anything which it takes hold of, but that fire is continually burning those who have once been seized by it, and never ceases; therefore also is it called unquenchable. For those also who have sinned must put on immortality, not for honor, but to have a constant supply of material for that punishment to work upon; and how terrible this is, speech could never depict, but from the experience of little things it is possible to form some slight notion of these great ones. For if you should ever be in a bath which has been heated more than it ought to be, think then, I beg you, on the fire of hell; or again, if you are ever inflamed by some severe fever, transfer your thoughts to that flame and then you will be able clearly to discern the difference. For if a bath and a fever so afflict and distress us, what will our condition be when we have fallen into that river of fire which winds in front of the terrible judgment seat. Then we shall gnash our teeth under the suffering of our labors and intolerable pains, but there will be no one to aid us. Yes, we shall groan mightily, as the flame is applied more severely to us, but we shall see no one except those who are being punished with us, and great desolation. And how should anyone describe the terrors arising to our souls from the darkness? For just as that fire has no consuming power, so neither has it any power of giving light, for otherwise there would not be darkness.

The dismay produced in us then by this, and the trembling and the great astonishment, can be sufficiently realized in that day only. For in that world many and various kinds of torment and torrents of punishment are poured in upon the soul from every side. And if anyone should ask, "And how can the soul bear up against such a multitude of punishments and continue being chastised through interminable ages," let him consider what happens in this world, how many have often born up against a long and severe disease. And if they have died, this has happened not because the soul was consumed but because the body was exhausted, so that had the latter not broken down, the soul would not have ceased being tormented. When then we have received an incorruptible and inconsumable body, there is nothing to prevent the punishment being indefinitely extended. For here indeed it is impossible that the two things should coexist—I mean severity of punishment and permanence—and cannot bear the concurrence of both; but when the imperishable state has supervened, these terrible things will keep their hold upon us for infinite time with much force. Let us not then so dispose ourselves now as if the excessive power of the tortures were destructive together with the soul, in a state of eternal punishment, and there will not be any end to look to beyond this.

I will not try now to convince you that luxury and pleasures are unpleasing, as you are not in a mindset that will allow you to see it that way. But let us assume it is all pleasurable, is it all worth eternal punishment? Our lives here are so short, like the blink of an eye, compared with eternity. This brief timeframe of struggling to do good yields a disproportionate, immeasurable eternal reward; consider how sinners will feel after this life, realizing that the passing pleasures they enjoyed were not worth the eternal affliction they are suffering and will continue to suffer from.

How much luxury then and how much time will you weigh in the balance against this punishment and vengeance? Do you propose a period of a hundred years or twice as long? And what is this compared with the endless ages? For what the dream of a single day is in the midst of a whole lifetime, that the enjoyment of things here is as contrasted with the state of things to come. Is there then anyone who, for the sake of seeing a good dream, would elect to be perpetually punished? Who is so senseless as to have recourse to this kind of retribution? For I am not yet accusing luxury nor revealing now the bitterness which lurks in it, for the present is not the proper time for these remarks, but when you have been able to escape it. For now, entangled as you are by this passion, you will suspect me of talking nonsense, if I were to call pleasure bitter, but when by the grace of God you have been released from the malady then you will know its misery full well. Wherefore, reserving these topics for another season, what I will say now is just this: be it so, that luxury is luxury, and pleasure, pleasure, and that they have nothing in them painful or disgraceful, what shall we say to the punishment which is in store for us?

And what shall we do then if we have taken our pleasure now, as it were in a shadow and a figure, but undergo everlasting torment there in reality, when we might in a short space of time escape these tortures already mentioned, and enjoy the good things which are stored up for us? For this also is the work of the loving-kindness of God, that our struggles are not protracted to a great length, but that after struggling for a brief, and tiny twinkling of an eye (for such is the present life compared with the other) we receive crowns of victory for endless ages.

And it will be no small affliction to the souls of those who are being punished at that time, to reflect that when they had it in their power in the few days of this life to make all good, they neglected their opportunity and surrendered themselves to everlasting evil. And lest we should suffer this, let us rouse ourselves while it is the accepted time, while it is the day of salvation,[1] while the power of repentance is great. For not only the evils already mentioned, but others also far worse than these await us if we are indolent. These indeed, and some more bitter than these, have their place in hell; but the loss of the good things involves so much pain, so much affliction and distress, that even if no other kind of punishment were appointed for those who sin here, it would of itself be sufficient to vex us more bitterly than the torments in hell, and to confound our souls.

---

1   2 Corinthians 6:2

Recognize the Splendor Which Awaits Us

I hope you truly consider what the afterlife will be like for those who are worthy of it, which we can attempt to understand from some passages in Scripture. The conditions of this life that burden us with sorrow will go away and give way to peace, gladness, joy, and heavenly light. But the greatest of all is that we can enjoy a perpetual relationship with Christ, in the company of His angels.

For I hope you consider the condition of the other life, so far as it is possible to consider it; for no words will suffice for an adequate description. But from the things which are told us, as if by means of certain riddles, let us try and get some indistinct vision of it. "Pain and sorrow and sighing," we read "have fled away."[1] What then could be more blessed than this life? It is not possible there to fear poverty and disease; it is not possible to see anyone injuring, or being injured, provoking, or being provoked, or angry, or envious, or burning with any outrageous lust, or anxious concerning the supply of the necessaries of life, or bemoaning himself over the loss of some dignity and power, for all the tempest of passion in us is quelled and brought to nothing, and all will be in a condition of peace, and gladness and joy, all things serene and tranquil, all will be daylight and brightness, and light—not this present light, but one excelling this in splendor as much as this excels the brightness of a lamp. For things are not concealed in that world by night, or by a gathering of clouds—bodies there are not set on fire and burned—for there is neither night nor evening there, nor cold nor heat, nor any other variation of seasons, but the condition is of a different kind, such as they only will know who have been deemed worthy of it. There is no old age there, nor any of the evils of old age, but all things relating to decay are utterly removed, and incorruptible glory reigns in every part. But greater than all these things is the perpetual enjoyment of interrelation with Christ in the company of angels, and archangels, and the higher powers.

Imagine passing beyond the sky to a place that is far more brilliant and beautiful than the beauty of the world you

---

1　Isaiah 35:10

behold in this life. After this life, as incorruptible souls, we will have to live in a world that likewise becomes incorruptible and more splendid, with no fear, no death or threat of death or hell, or any such terror; rather, we, as with all the saints, will shed off our lowly state to exist in a dignified, lofty condition.

Behold now the sky, and pass through it in thought to the region beyond the sky, and consider the transfiguration to take place in the whole creation; for it will not continue to be such as it is now, but will be far more brilliant and beautiful; and just as gold glistens more brightly than lead, so will the future constitution of the universe be better than the present, even as the blessed Paul says, "Because the creation also itself shall be delivered from the bondage of corruption."[2] For now indeed, seeing that it partakes of corruption, it is subject to many things such as bodies of this kind naturally experience; but then, having divested itself of all these things, we shall see it display its beauty in an incorruptible form, for inasmuch as it is to receive incorruptible bodies, it will in the future be itself also transfigured into the more noble condition. Nowhere in that world will there be sedition and strife, for great is the concord of the band of saints, all being ever in harmony with one another. It is not possible there to fear the devil, and the plots of demons, or the threatenings of hell, or death, either that death which now is, or the other death which is far worse than this, but every terror of this kind will have been done away. And just as some royal child, who

---

2   Romans 8:21

has been brought up in modest semblance, and subject to fear and threats, lest he should deteriorate by indulgence and become unworthy of his paternal inheritance, as soon as he has attained the royal dignity, immediately exchanges all his former raiment for the purple robe, and the diadem and the crowd of bodyguards, and assumes his state with much confidence, having cast out of his soul thoughts of humility and subjection, and having taken others in their place, even so will it happen then to all the saints.

> The transfiguration of Christ gave us a glimpse of the more lofty life awaiting us, but what was seen was limited by what mortal eyes were able to comprehend; to truly be capable of seeing the full splendor of the world to come, one must see it with immortal eyes.

And to prove that these words are no empty boast, let us journey in thought to the mountain where Christ was transfigured; let us behold Him shining as He shone there; and yet even then He did not display to us all the splendor of the world to come. For that the vision was accommodated to human eyes, and not an exact manifestation of the reality, is plain from the very words of the evangelist. For what does he say? "He did shine as the Sun."[3] But the glory of incorruptible bodies does not emit the same kind of light as this body which is corruptible, nor is it of a kind to be tolerable to mortal eyes, but needs

---

3   Matthew 17:2

incorruptible and immortal eyes to contemplate it. But at that time on the mountain He disclosed to them as much as it was possible for them to see without injuring the sight of the beholders, and even so they could not endure it but fell upon their faces.

> Tell me, if someone brought you into a place full of light, where everyone seated was arrayed in the most splendid apparel and donned crowns on their heads, and then you were promised you could join their ranks, would you not do everything to obtain that? We have before us something even greater, beyond our imagination, where we would be in the company of angels, and have the ability to gaze upon Christ in His splendor and be counted among the saints, so what would you not be willing to endure in order to take part in that?

Tell me, if anyone led you into some bright place, where all were sitting arrayed in vestures of gold, and amid the multitude pointed out one other to you who alone had garments wrought with precious stones, and a crown upon his head, and then promised to place you in the ranks of these people, would you not do everything to obtain this promise? Open then even now in imagination your eyes, and look on that assembly, composed not of men such as we are, but of those who are of more value than gold and precious stones, and the beams of the sun, and all visible radiance, and not consisting of men only but of beings of much more dignity than men: angels, archangels, thrones, dominions, principalities, powers. For as concerning the king it is not even possible to say what he is like, so completely do his beauty, his grace, his splendor, his glory, his grandeur and magnificence elude speech and thought. Shall we then, I ask, deprive ourselves of such great blessings, in order to avoid suffering for a brief period? For if we had to endure countless deaths every day, or even hell itself, for the sake of seeing Christ coming in His glory, and being enrolled in the company of the saints, ought we not to undergo all those things? Hear what the blessed Peter says: "It is good for us to be here."[4] But if he, when he beheld some dim image of the things to come, immediately cast away all other things out of his soul on account of the pleasure produced in it by that vision, what would anyone say when the actual reality of the things are presented, when the palace is thrown open and it is permitted to gaze upon the King Himself, no longer darkly, or by means of a mirror,[5] but face to face, no longer by means of faith, but by sight?

---

4   Matthew 17:4

5   1 Corinthians 13:12

Desire Heaven Instead of Just Escaping Hell

Most are motivated by the desire to escape hell, but exclusion from the glory of heaven should be seen as far worse than the miseries of hell. Imagine the majesty of a royal king and the extent to which people wish to be counted among his company, how much more ought we to yearn for the superior splendor of our heavenly King?

The majority, it is true, of those who are not very sensibly minded, propose to be content with escaping hell, but I say that a far more severe punishment than hell is exclusion from the glory of the other world, and I think that one who has failed to reach it ought not to sorrow so much over the miseries of hell, as over his rejection from heaven, for this alone is more dreadful than all other things with respect to punishment. But frequently now when we see a king, attended by a large bodyguard, enter the palace, we count those happy who are near him, and have a share in his speech and mind, and partake of all the rest of his glory; and even if we have countless blessings, we have no perception of any of them, and deem ourselves miserable when we look at the glory of those who are round about him, although we know that such splendor is slippery and insecure, both on account of wars, and plots, and envy, and because apart from these things it is not in itself worthy of any consideration. But where the King of all is concerned, He who holds not a portion of the earth but the whole circuit of it, or rather who comprehends it all in the hollow of His hand, and measures the heavens with a span, who upholds all things by the word of His power,[1] by whom all the nations are counted as nothing, and as a drop of spit, in the case of such a king, I say, shall we not reckon it the most extreme punishment to miss being enrolled in that company which is round about Him, but be content if we merely escape hell? And what could be more pitiable than this condition of soul?

The heavenly King, for whom we should yearn to be counted among His majestic splendor, comes with power and might: the world will be shaken, accompanied by frightful wonders, and mankind shall be subject to His

---

1   Hebrews 1:3; much of the other expressions describing God in this section are taken from Isaiah 40.

judgment.

For this King does not come to judge the earth, drawn by a pair of white mules, nor riding in a golden chariot, nor arrayed in a purple robe and diadem. How then does He come? Hear the prophets crying aloud and saying as much as it is possible to tell to men, for one says, "God shall come openly, even our God, and shall not keep silence; a fire shall be kindled before Him, and a mighty tempest shall be round about Him; He shall call heaven from above and the earth that He may judge His people."[2] But Isaiah depicts the actual punishment impending over us, speaking thus: "Behold the day of the Lord comes, inexorable, with wrath and anger, to lay the whole world desolate, and to destroy sinners out of it. For the stars of heaven, and Orion, and the whole system of heaven shall not give their light, and the sun shall be darkened in its going down, and the moon shall not give her light; and I will ordain evils against the whole world, and visit their sins upon the ungodly, and I will destroy the insolence of the lawless, and humble the insolence of the proud, and they who are left shall be more precious than unsmelted gold, and a man shall be more precious than the sapphire stone. For heaven shall be disturbed and the earth shall be shaken from its foundations by reason of the fury of the wrath of the Lord of Sabaoth, in the day when His wrath shall come upon us."[3] And again "windows" he says "shall be opened from

---

2   Psalm 50:3–4

3   Isaiah 13:9–13

heaven, and the foundations of the earth shall be shaken; the earth shall be mightily confounded, the earth shall be bent low, it shall be perplexed with great perplexity, the earth shall stagger grievously like the drunkard and the reveler, the earth shall shake as a hut, it shall fall and not be able to rise up again, for iniquity has increased mightily there. And God shall set His hand upon the host of heaven on high in that day, and upon the kingdoms of the earth, and He shall gather together the congregation thereof into a prison, and shall shut them up in a stronghold."[4]

And Malachi speaking concordantly with these said: "Behold the Lord Almighty comes, and who shall abide on the day of His coming or who shall stand when He appears? For He comes like a refiner's fire, and like launderer's soap; and He shall sit refining and purifying as it were silver, and as it were gold."[5] And again, "behold," he says, "the day of the Lord comes, burning like an oven, and it shall consume them, and all the aliens, and all who work iniquity shall be stubble, and the day which is coming shall set fire to them, says the Lord Almighty; and there shall be left neither root nor branch."[6]

And the man greatly beloved[7] says, "I beheld until thrones were placed, and the Ancient of Days was seated, and His raiment was white as snow, and the hair of His head was pure as wool. His throne was a flame of fire, and its wheels a burning fire; a stream of fire wound its way

---

4   Isaiah 24:18–22

5   Malachi 3:1–3

6   Malachi 4:1

7   In Daniel's vision, he was called "man greatly beloved" (Daniel 10:11).

in front of Him. Thousand thousands ministered unto Him, and ten thousand times ten thousand stood before Him. The judgment was set and the books were opened."[8] Then after a little space "I beheld," he says, "in a vision of the night, and behold, with the clouds of heaven, one came like the Son of Man, and reached unto the Ancient of Days, and was brought near before Him, and to Him was given rule, and honor, and the kingdom, and all the people, tribes and tongues serve Him. His dominion is an everlasting dominion, which shall not pass away, and His kingdom shall not be destroyed. As for me Daniel, my spirit shuddered within me, and the visions of my head troubled me."[9]

Then all the gates of the heavenly vaults are opened, or rather the heaven itself is taken away out of the midst "for heaven," we read "shall be rolled up like a scroll,"[10] wrapped up in the middle like the skin and covering of some tent so as to be transformed into some better shape. Then all things are full of amazement and horror and trembling; then even the angels themselves are held by much fear, and not angels only but also archangels and thrones, and dominions, and principalities and authorities. "For the powers" we read "of the heavens shall be shaken," because their fellow-servants are required to give an account of their life in this world.[11] For if when a single city is being judged before rulers in this world, all men shudder, even those who are outside the

---

8   Daniel 7:9–10

9   Daniel 7:13–15

10   Isaiah 34:4

11   Matthew 24:29

danger, [then] when the whole world is arraigned before such a judge as this who needs no witnesses, or proofs, but independently of all these things brings forward deeds and words and thoughts, and exhibits them all as in some picture both to those who have committed the sins and to those who are ignorant of them, how is it not natural that every power should be confounded and shake? For if there were no river of fire winding by, nor any terrible angels standing by the side of the throne, but men were merely summoned, some to be praised and admired, others to be dismissed with ignominy that they might not see the glory of God ("for let the ungodly" we read "be taken away that he may not see the glory of the Lord"),[12] and if this were the only punishment, would not the loss of such blessings sting the souls of those who were deprived of them more bitterly than all hell itself? For how great an evil this is cannot possibly be represented now in words; but then we shall know it clearly in the actual reality. But now, I earnestly plea, add the punishment also to the scene, and imagine men not only covered with shame, and veiling their heads, and bending them low, but also being dragged along the road to the fire, and hauled away to the instruments of torture and delivered over to the cruel powers, and suffering these things just at the time when all they who have practiced what is good, and wrought deeds worthy of eternal life, are being crowned, and proclaimed conquerors, and presented before the royal throne.

---

12   Isaiah 26:10

Unfathomable Happiness in God's Embrace

No language can describe the joy of being in Christ's presence. Think of the pleasure people feel over temporary, physical things in this passing world, and then contrast that with the unfathomable level of happiness people will feel as they experience the indescribable, unimaginable, permanent splendor of heaven.

Now these are things which will happen in that day, but the things which will follow, after these, what language can describe to us the pleasure, the profit, the joy of being in the company of Christ? For when the soul has returned to the proper condition of nobility, and is able from then on with much boldness to behold its Master, it is impossible to say what great pleasure it derives, what great gain, rejoicing not only in the good things actually in hand, but in the belief that these things will never come to an end.

All that gladness then cannot be described in words, nor grasped by understanding, but in an obscure kind of way, as one indicates great things by means of small ones, I will endeavor to make it manifest. For let us scrutinize those who enjoy the good things of the world in this present life—I mean wealth and power—and how they take great pleasure in it; exulting with delight, they reckon themselves as no longer being upon the earth, and this although the things which they are enjoying are acknowledged not to be really good, and do not abide with them, but take to flight more quickly than a dream. And even if they should even last for a little time, their favor is displayed within the limits of this present life, and cannot accompany us further.

Now if these things uplift those who possess them to such a level of joy, what do you suppose is the condition of those souls which are invited to enjoy the countless blessings in heaven which are always securely fixed and stable? And not only this, but also in their quantity and quality they exceed present things to such an extent as never entered even the heart of man.[1] For at the present time, like an infant in the womb, even so do we dwell in this world confined in a narrow space, and are unable to behold the splendor and the freedom of the world to come; but when the time of travail arrives and the present

---

1   Isaiah 64:4, which is also quoted in 1 Corinthians 2:9

life is delivered at the day of judgment of all men whom it has contained, those who have been miscarried go from darkness into darkness, and from affliction into more grievous affliction, but those who are perfectly formed and have preserved the marks of the royal image will be presented to the King, and will take upon themselves that service which angels and archangels minister to the God of all.

> God mercifully has given us no control over natural beauty, so that we are not preoccupied with such vanity, but instead has given us full control, with His grace, to make our spirits beautiful. Even then, look at how much effort we put into coming up with all sorts of ways to beautify our bodies (such as makeup, penciling eyebrows, clothing arrangements, hair styling). Now imagine if God gave us the power to reshape and transform our bodies as we wished, think of how obssessed we would be with this, and how much more we would neglect our souls!

I implore you then, O friend, do not finally efface these marks, but speedily restore them, and stamp them more perfectly on your soul. For corporeal beauty indeed God has confined within the limits of nature, but grace of soul is released from the constraint and bondage arising from such, to the extent that it is far superior to any bodily similarity, and it depends entirely upon ourselves and the grace of God.

For our Master, being merciful, has in this special way

honored our race, that He has entrusted to nature the unavoidable, inferior things which contribute nothing much to our advantage, the outcome of which are matters of unimportance, but of the things which are really noble He has caused us to be ourselves the crafter. For if He had placed corporeal beauty also under our control we should have been subjected to excessive anxiety, and should have wasted all our time upon things which are of no profit, and should have grievously neglected our soul.

For if, even as it is, when we have not this power in ourselves, we make intense efforts, and give ourselves up to shadow painting, and because we cannot in reality produce bodily beauty, we cunningly devise imitations by means of paints, and dyes, and dressing of hair, and arrangement of garments, and penciling of eyebrows, and many other contrivances, what leisure should we have set apart for the soul and serious matters, if we had it in our power to transfigure the body into a really symmetrical shape? For probably, if this were our business, we should not have any other, but should spend all our time upon it, adorning the bondmaid with countless decorations, but letting her who is the mistress of this bondmaid lie perpetually in a state of deformity and neglect. For this reason God, having delivered us from this vain occupation, implanted in us the power of working upon the nobler element, and he who cannot turn an ugly body into a comely one, can raise the soul, even when it has been reduced to the extremity of ugliness, to the very highest point of grace, and make it so amiable and desirable that not only are good men brought to long after it but even He who is the sovereign and God of all, even as the Psalmist also when discoursing concerning this beauty said, "And the king shall have desire of your beauty."[2]

> If even according to earthly human standards men may be willing to overlook the actions of a prostitute and marry her if she happens to be extremely attractive, how much more would God be willing to have pity on our souls despite our fall? The allegory of a promiscuous bride (symbolizing our soul) who is still loved and wanted by her Bridegroom (God) despite her actions can be found throughout Scripture. Such enduring love can only be found in God.

Do you not see also that in the houses of prostitutes the women who are ugly and shameless would hardly be accepted by prize-fighters, and runaway slaves, and gladiators, but should any attractive, well-born and modest woman, owing to some misfortune, have been reduced to this necessity, no man, even among those who are very illustrious and great, would be ashamed of marriage with her? Now if there is so much pity among men, and so much disdain of glory as to release from that bondage the women who have often been disgraced in the brothel, and to place them in the position of wives, much more is this the case with God, and those souls which, owing to the usurpation of the devil, have fallen from their original noble condition into the harlotry of this present life.

---

2   Psalm 45:11

And you will find the prophets filled with examples of this kind, when they address Jerusalem, for she fell into fornication, and a novel form of it, even as Ezekiel says: "To all harlots wages are given, but you have given wages to your lovers, and there has been perversion in you beyond all other women";[3] and again another says, "You did sit waiting for them like a deserted bird."[4] This one then who has committed fornication in this fashion God calls back again. For the captivity which took place was not so much by way of vengeance as for the purpose of conversion and correction, since if God had wished to punish them outright He would not again have brought them back to their home; He would not have established their city and their temple in greater splendor than before: "For the final glory of this house," He said, "shall exceed the former."[5] Now if God did not exclude from repentance her who had many times committed fornication, much more will He embrace my soul, which has now fallen for the first time. For certainly there is no lover of corporeal beauty, even if he be very frantic, who is so inflamed with the love of his mistress as God longs after the salvation of our souls; and both of these we may perceive from the divine Scriptures.

See at least, both in the introduction of Jeremiah, and many other places of the prophets, when He is despised and treated with contempt, how He again hastens forward and pursues the friendship of those who turn away from Him, which also He Himself made clear in the Gospels saying,

---

3   Ezekiel 16:33

4   Jeremiah 3:2

5   Haggai 2:9

"O Jerusalem! Jerusalem! The one who kills the prophets and stones them that are sent to you, how often would I have gathered your children together even as a hen gathers her chicken under her wings, and you were not willing?"[6] And Paul writing to the Corinthians said "that God was in Christ reconciling the world unto Himself, not reckoning their trespasses unto them, and has committed unto us the word of reconciliation. We are ambassadors therefore on behalf of Christ, as though God were entreating by us; we beseech you on behalf of Christ, be reconciled to God."[7] Consider that this has now been said to us. For it is not merely a lack of faith, but also an unclean life which is sufficient to work this abominate enmity. "For the carnal mind" we read "is enmity against God."[8] Let us then break down the barrier, and hew it in pieces, and destroy it, that we may enjoy the blessed reconciliation, that we may become again the fondly beloved of God.

---

6   Matthew 23:37

7   2 Corinthians 5:19–20

8   Romans 8:7

Our Spirit's Beauty Far Exceeds the Physical

I know you are so focused on how attractive Hermione looks and your heart is in a flurry of excitement, but if you really think about what you are attracted to—a physical body that is just full of fluid, food, bile, spit, and other such things—you would hopefully realize what you admire is far less beautiful than one's soul.

I know that you are now admiring the grace of Hermione, and you judge that there is nothing in the world to be compared to her attractiveness; but if you choose, O friend, you shall yourself exceed her in beauty and gracefulness, as much as golden statues surpass those which are made of clay.

For if beauty, when it occurs in the body, so fascinates and excites the minds of most men, when the soul is shining brightly with it, what can match beauty and grace of this kind? For the groundwork of this corporeal beauty is nothing else but phlegm, and blood, and humor, and bile, and the fluid of masticated food.[1] For by these things both eyes and cheeks, and all the other features, are supplied with moisture; and if they do not receive that moisture, daily ascending from the stomach and the liver, the skin becoming unduly withered, and the eyes sunken, the whole grace of the countenance immediately vanishes, so that if you consider what is stored up inside those beautiful eyes, and that straight nose, and the mouth and the cheeks, you will affirm the well-shaped body to be nothing else than a whited sepulcher: the parts within are full of so much uncleanness. Moreover when you see a rag with any of these things on it, such as phlegm, or spit, you cannot bear to touch it with even the tips of your fingers, or rather, you cannot even endure looking at it; and yet are you in a flutter of excitement about the storehouses and depositories of these things?

The beauty of your soul so far exceeds physical beauty, as heaven is superior to earth.

1   St. John Chrysostom is here referring to the manner by which the body was understood at the time, based on a concept known as "the four humors." While its origins may have been derived from ancient Egypt, the famed Greek physician Hippocrates (460–370 BC) developed it into a medical theory, which associated certain moods, emotions, and behaviors with an excess or lack of bodily fluids: blood, yellow bile, black bile, and phlegm.

But your beauty was not of this kind, but excelled it as heaven is superior to earth; or rather, it was much better and more brilliant than this, for no one has anywhere seen a soul by itself, stripped of the body; but yet even so I will endeavor to present to you the beauty of this soul from another source. I mean, from the case of the greater powers hear at least how the beauty of these struck the man greatly beloved;[2] for wishing to describe their beauty, and being unable to find a body of the same character, he had recourse to metallic substances, and he was not satisfied even with these, but took the brilliancy of lightning for his illustration.[3] Now if those powers, even when they did not disclose their essential nature pure and bare, but only in a very dim and shadowy way, nevertheless shone so brightly, what must their appearance naturally be, when set free from every veil? Now we ought to form some such image of the beauty of the soul. "For they shall be," we read, "equal to the angels."[4]

Now in the case of bodies, the lighter and finer kinds, and those which have retreated to the path which tend towards the incorporeal, they are very much better and more wonderful than the others. The sky at least is more beautiful than the earth, and fire than water, and the stars than precious stones; and we admire the rainbow far more than violets and roses, and all other flowers which are upon the earth. And in short, if it were possible with bodily eyes

---

2   This is in reference to Daniel's vision, as Daniel was called "man greatly beloved" (Daniel 10:11).

3   Daniel 10:6

4   Luke 20:36

to behold the beauty of the soul, you would laugh to scorn these corporeal illustrations; so feebly have they presented to us the gracefulness of the soul.

> **Do not neglect the beauty of your soul, which is worth tolerating affliction to maintain.**

Let us not then neglect such a possession, nor such great happiness, and especially when the approach to that kind of beauty becomes easy to us by our hopes of the things to come. "For our light affliction" we read, "which is but for the moment, works for us more and more exceedingly an eternal weight of glory, while we look not at the things which are seen but at the things which are not seen; for the things which are seen are temporal, but the things which are not seen are eternal."[5] Now if the blessed Paul called such afflictions as you know of light and easy, because he did not look at the things which are seen, much more tolerable is it merely to cease from wantonness. For we are not calling you to those dangers which he underwent, nor to those deaths which he incurred daily:[6] the constant beatings and scourgings, the bonds, the enmity of the whole world, the hatred of his own people, the frequent vigils, the long journeys, the shipwrecks, the attacks of robbers, the plots of his own kinsfolk, the distresses on account of his friends, the hunger, the cold, the nakedness,

---

5   2 Corinthians 4:17–18

6   1 Corinthians 15:31; 2 Corinthians 11:23–28

the burning, the despondency on account both of those who belonged to him, and those who did not belong to him.

> Release yourself from bondage and return to your former freedom, remembering the punishment that is the consequence for a life of spiritual recklessness. It makes no sense that Christians who know the consequences of remaining in sin would stay cast down when they fall into temptation, while non-Christians in everyday life would not beat themselves up when they feel defeated, but would keep fighting. For example, when a boxer fights, if he falls, would he start punching himself, or would he instead get up and keep fighting his opponent? The example of David teaches us the benefit of getting up again despite falling into sins such as you have fallen into.

None of these things do we now demand of you; all that we ask for is that you would release yourself from your accursed bondage, and return to your former freedom, having considered both the punishment arising from your wantonness, and the honor belonging to your former manner of life. For that unbelievers should be but languidly affected by the thought of the resurrection and never be in fear of this kind, is nothing wonderful; but that we who are more firmly persuaded concerning the things of the other world than those of the present should spend our life in this miserable and deplorable way, and be nowise affected by the memory of those things, but sink into a state of extreme insensibility—this is irrational in the highest degree. For when we who believe do the deeds of unbelievers, or rather are in a more miserable plight than they (for there are some among them who have been eminent for the virtue of their life), what consolation, what excuse will be left for us? And many merchants indeed who have incurred shipwreck have not given way, but have pursued the same journey, and this when the loss which has befallen them was not owing to their own carelessness, but to the force of the winds; and shall we who have reason to be confident concerning the end, and know certainly that if we do not wish it, neither shipwreck nor accident of any kind will bring us damage, [shall we] not lay hold of the work again, and carry on our business as we did in the past? Or should we instead lie in idleness and keep our hands to ourselves; and if we were to have kept them merely to ourselves, and not use them against ourselves, [this would be] a token of stark madness; for if any boxer, leaving his opponent, were to turn his hands against his own head, and deal blows to his own face, should we not, I ask, rank him among madmen?

For the devil has upset us and cast us down; therefore we ought to get up, and not to be dragged down again and precipitate ourselves, and add blows dealt by ourselves to the blows dealt by him. For the blessed David also had a fall like that which has now happened to you; and not this only but another also which followed it—I mean that of murder. What then? Did he remain prostrate? Did he not immediately rise up again with energy and place himself in position to fight the enemy? In fact, he wrestled with him so bravely, that even after his death he was the protector of his offspring. For when Solomon had perpetrated great iniquity, and had deserved countless deaths, God said that He would leave him the kingdom intact, thus speaking: "I will surely rend the kingdom out of your hand and will give it to your servant. Nevertheless I will not do this in your days." For what reason? "For David your father's sake, I will take it out of the hand of your son."[7] And again when Hezekiah was about to run the greatest possible risk, although he was a righteous man, God said that He would succor him for the sake of this saint. "For I will cast My shield," He says, "over this city to save it for My own sake, and for My servant David's sake."[8] So great is the force of repentance.

But if he had determined with himself, as you do now, that henceforth it was impossible to propitiate God—and if he had said within himself, "God has honored me with great honor, and has given me a place among the prophets, and has entrusted me with the government of my countrymen, and rescued me out of countless perils, how then, when I have offended against Him after such great benefits, and have perpetrated the worst crimes, shall I be able to recover His favor?"—if he had thought thus, not only would he not have done the things which he afterwards did, but he would have aggravated his former evils.

---

7 1 Kings 11:11–12

8 2 Kings 19:34

God Yearns to Reward Us, Not to Punish Us

In the case of physical illness, even if doctors tell us it is beyond hope, we do all we can to save the body. But on the other hand, when it comes to the spirit and its maladies, for which recovery is never beyond reach, we plunge into despair as if there is nothing we can do. Focusing on your spirit more than your body will *save* both; focusing on just the body will cause you to *lose* both.

For not only the bodily wounds work death, if they are neglected, but also those of the soul; and yet we have arrived at such a level of foolishness as to take the greatest care of the former, and to overlook the latter. And although in the case of the body it naturally often happens that many wounds are incurable, yet we do not abandon hope, but even when we hear the physicians constantly declaring that it is not possible to get rid of this suffering by medicines, we still persist in exhorting them to devise at least some slight alleviation; but in the case of souls, where there is no incurable malady—for it is not subject to the necessity of nature—here, as if the infirmities were strange, we are negligent and despairing. And where the nature of the [physical] disorder might naturally plunge us into despair, we take as much pains as if there were great hope of restoration to health; but where [for the soul] there is no occasion to renounce hope, we desist from efforts, and become as heedless as if matters were desperate; so much more account do we take of the body than of the soul. And this is the reason why we are not able to save even the body. For he who neglects the leading element, and manifests all his zeal about inferior matters, destroys and loses both; whereas he who observes the right order, and preserves and cherishes the more commanding element, even if he neglects the secondary element, yet preserves it by means of saving the primary one. This also Christ signified to us when He said, "Fear not those who kill the body, but are not able to kill the soul; but rather fear Him who is able to destroy both soul and body in hell."[1]

Well, do I convince you that one ought never to despair of the disorders of the soul as incurable? Or must I again set other arguments in motion? For even if you should despair of yourself ten thousand times, I will never despair of you, and I will never myself be guilty of that for

---

1   Matthew 10:28

which I reproach others; and yet it is not the same thing for a man to renounce hope for himself, as for another to renounce hope for him. For he who has this suspicion concerning another may readily obtain pardon, but he who has it of himself will not. Why so? Because the one has no controlling power over the zeal and repentance of the other, but over his own zeal and repentance a man has sole authority. Nevertheless, even so I will not despair of you, though you should any number of times be affected in this way; for it may be that there will be some return to virtue, and to restoration to your former manner of life.

Despair is unjustified. The Ninevites who may have had reason to believe there was no hope nonetheless recognized God's mercy.

And now hear what follows. The Ninevites, when they heard the prophet vehemently declaring and plainly threatening, "Yet three days and Nineveh shall be overthrown,"[2] even then did not lose heart, but, although they had no confidence that they should be able to move the mind of God, or rather had reason to suspect the contrary from the divine message (for the utterance was not accompanied by any qualification, but was a simple declaration), even then they manifested repentance saying: "Who knows whether God will relent and be entreated,

---

2   Jonah 3:4; note, according to the Septuagint the number of days declared to Nineveh are three, rather than forty.

and turn from the fierceness of His wrath, and that we do not perish? And God saw their works, that they turned from their evil ways, and God relented of the evil which He said He would do to them and He did it not."[3] Now if barbarian and unreasoning men could perceive so much, much more ought we to do this who have been trained in the divine doctrines and have seen such a crowd of examples of this kind both in history and actual experience. "For My counsels" we read "are not as your counsels nor My ways as your ways; but as far as is heaven from the earth, so far are My thoughts from your mind, and My counsels from your counsels."[4] Now if we admit to our favor household servants when they have often offended against us, on their promising to become better, and place them again in their former position, and sometimes even grant them greater freedom of speech than before, much more does God act thus.

> God created us not to punish us, but to shower us with everlasting blessings. It is not your sin that will provoke God as much as your unwillingness to repent. He who is anxious to be loved by us does everything He can to motivate us to love Him and receive our due rewards; how then would He not welcome and love us when we repent?

For if God had made us in order to punish us, you might

---

3   Jonah 3:9–10

4   Isaiah 55:8–9

well have despaired and questioned the possibility of your own salvation. But if He created us for no other reason than His own good will, and with a view to our enjoying everlasting blessings, and if He does and contrives everything for this end, from the first day until the present time, what is there which can ever cause you to doubt? Have we provoked Him severely, so as no other man ever did? This is just the reason why we ought especially to abstain from our present deeds and to repent for the past, and exhibit a great change. For the evils we have once perpetrated cannot provoke Him so much as our being unwilling to make any change in the future. For to sin may be a merely human failing, but to continue in the same sin ceases to be human, and becomes altogether devilish. For observe how God by the mouth of His prophet blames this more than the other. "For," we read, "I said to her after she had done all these deeds of fornication, 'Return to Me,' and yet she returned not."[5] And again, from another quarter, when wishing to show the great longing which He has for our salvation, having heard how the people promised after many transgressions to tread the right way, He said: "Who will grant to them to have such a heart as to fear Me, and to keep My commandments all their days, that it may be well with them and with their children forever?"[6] And Moses when reasoning with them said, "And now, O Israel, what does the Lord your God require of you, but to fear the Lord your God, and to walk in all His ways, and

---

5   Jeremiah 3:7

6   Deuteronomy 5:29

to love Him?"[7]

He then who is so anxious to be loved by us, and does everything for this end, and did not spare even His only begotten Son on account of His love towards us, and who counts it a desirable thing if at any time we become reconciled to Himself, how shall He not welcome and love us when we repent? Hear at least what He says by the mouth of the prophet: "Declare first your iniquities that you may be justified."[8] Now this He demands from us in order to intensify our love towards Him. For when one who loves, after enduring many insults at the hands of those who are beloved, even then does not extinguish his fondness for them; the only reason why he takes pains to make those insults public is that by displaying the strength of his affection he may induce them to feel a larger and warmer love. Now if the confession of sins brings so much consolation, much more does the endeavor to wash them away by means of our deeds. For if this was not the case, but those who had once swerved from the straight path were forbidden to return to it again, perhaps no one, except a few persons whose numbers would be easily reckoned, would ever enter the kingdom of heaven; but as it is we shall find the most distinguished among those who have fallen. For those who have exhibited much vehemence in evil things, will also in turn exhibit the same in good things, being conscious what great debts they have incurred, which Christ also declared when He spoke to Simon concerning the woman: "'For you see this woman?

---

7   Deuteronomy 10:12

8   Isaiah 43:26

I entered into your house, you gave Me no water for My feet; be she has washed My feet with her tears and wiped them with the hairs of her head. You gave Me no kiss, but she since the time I came in has not ceased to kiss My feet. My head with oil you did not anoint, but she has anointed My feet with ointment. Wherefore I say unto you: her sins which are many are forgiven, for she loved much; but to whom little is forgiven, the same loves little.' And He said unto her, 'Your sins are forgiven.'"⁹

---

9   Luke 7:44–48

Just Begin Your Return &
Be a Role Model

What is difficult is getting yourself to start to repent,
but after that first step people often intensely pursue
full repentance, and the devil who has been defeated
eases off, making it easier to live a more virtuous life
with renewed energy. So let us quickly return to God and
hasten to arrive at our heavenly city.

For this reason also the devil, knowing that they who have
committed great evils, when they have begun to repent
do this with much zeal, inasmuch as they are conscious of
their offenses, fears and trembles lest they should make a
beginning of the work; for after they have made it they are
no longer capable of being checked, and, kindling like fire

under the influence of repentance, they render their souls purer than pure gold, being impelled by their conscience, and the memory of their former sins, as by some strong gale, towards the haven of virtue. And this is the point in which they have an advantage over those who have never fallen, that they exercise more vehement energy, if only, as I said, they can lay hold of the beginning. For the task which is hard and difficult of accomplishment is to be able to set foot on the entrance, and to reach the vestibule of repentance, and to repulse and overthrow the enemy there when he is fiercely raging and assaulting us. But after this, he will not display so much fury when he has once been worsted, and has fallen where he was strong; and we shall receive greater energy, and shall run this good race with much ease.

Let us then from now on set about our return, let us hasten up to the city which is in heaven, in which we have been enrolled, in which also we have been appointed to find our home as citizens. For to despair of ourselves not only has this evil—that it shuts the gates of that city against us, and that it drives us into greater indolence and contempt—but also that it plunges us into satanic recklessness. For the only cause why the devil became such as he is was that he first of all despaired, and afterwards from despair sank into recklessness. For the soul, when once it has abandoned its own salvation, will no longer perceive that it is plunging downwards, choosing to do and say everything which is adverse to its own salvation. And just as madmen, when once they have fallen out of a sound condition, are neither afraid nor ashamed of anything, but fearlessly dare all manner of things, even if they have to fall into fire, or deep water, or down a precipice, so they who have been seized by the frenzy of despair are hence forward unmanageable, rushing into vice in every direction, and if death does not come to put a stop to this madness and vehemence, they do themselves infinite harm.

> **I beg you to please return to your senses and get back up again. Even if you repent and have to gradually recover to where you once were, simply entering on the path of repentance will allow you to lay hold on eternal life and serve as a role model for everyone who may actually be stumbling now because of your bad example. Those who come back from a sinful life through repentance often shine more brightly than those who have never fallen as low.**

Therefore I entreat you, before you are deeply steeped in this drunkenness, recover your senses and rouse yourself up, and shake off this satanic fit, doing it gently and gradually if it be not possible to effect it all at once. For to me indeed the easier course seems to be to wrench yourself once for all out of all the cords which hold you down, and transfer yourself to the school of repentance. But if this seems to you a difficult thing, that you should be willing to enter on the path which leads to better things, simply enter upon it, and lay hold on eternal life. Yes I beseech and implore you by your former reputation, by that confidence which once was yours, let us see you once again standing on the pinnacle of virtue, and in the same condition of perseverance as before.

Spare those who are made to stumble on your account, those who are falling, who are becoming more indolent, who are despairing of the way of virtue. For dejection now holds possession of the band of brethren, while pleasure and cheerfulness prevail in the councils of the unbelieving, and of those young men who are disposed to indolence. But if you return again to your former strictness of life, the result will be reversed, and all our shame will be transferred to them, while we shall enjoy much confidence, seeing you again crowned and proclaimed victor with more splendor than before, for such victories bring greater renown and pleasure. For you will not only receive the reward of your own achievements, but also of the exhortation and consolation of others, being exhibited as a striking model, if ever anyone should fall into the same condition, to encourage him to get up and recover himself.

Do not neglect such an opportunity of gain, nor drag our souls down into Hades with sorrow, but let us breathe freely again, and shake off the cloud of despondency which oppresses us on your account. For now, passing by the consideration of our own troubles, we mourn over your calamities, but if you are willing to come to your senses, and see clearly, and to join the angelic host, you will release us from this sorrow, and will take away the greater part of sins.

For that it is possible for those who have come back again after repentance to shine with much luster, and oftentimes more than those who have never fallen at all, I have demonstrated from the divine writings. Thus at least both the publicans and the harlots inherit the kingdom of heaven; thus many of the last are placed before the first.

Actual Stories of People Returning to God

I will tell you about real life stories that have happened in our lifetime, that you may have heard about, of people who tragically abandoned godliness yet returned: A rich orphan who forsook Christianity, and a monk who suddenly fell into desire for women.

But I will tell you also of events which have happened in our own time, and of which you may yourself have been witness. You know probably that young Phoenician, the son of Urbanus, who was untimely left an orphan, but possessed much money, and many servants and lands. This man, having in the first place bidden complete farewell to his studies in the schools, and having laid aside the showy clothing which he formerly wore, and all his worldly grandeur, suddenly arraying himself in a shabby cloak, and retreating to the solitude of the mountains, exhibited a high degree of Christian philosophy not merely in proportion to his age, but such as any great and wonderful man might have displayed. And after this, having been deemed worthy of initiation into the sacred mysteries, he made still greater advances in virtue. And all were rejoicing, and glorifying God, that one nurtured in wealth, and having illustrious ancestors, and being still a mere youth, should have suddenly trodden all the pomps of this life underfoot, and ascended to the true height.

Now while he was in this condition, and an object of admiration, certain corrupt men, who according to the law of kindred had oversight of him, dragged him back again into the former sea of worldliness. And so, having flung aside all his habits, he again descended from the mountains into the midst of the forum, and used to go all round the city, riding on horseback, and accompanied by a large retinue; and he was no longer willing to live even soberly, for being inflamed by much luxury, he was constrained to fall into foolish love intrigues, and there was no one of those conversant with him who did not despair of his salvation; he was encompassed by such a swarm of flatterers, besides the snares of orphanhood, youth, and great wealth. And persons who readily find fault with everything accused those who originally conducted him to this way of life,[1] saying that he had both missed his spiritual aims and would no longer be of any use in the management of his

---

1   i.e., the life of monastic seclusion.

own affairs, having prematurely abandoned the labors of study, and having been consequently unable to derive any benefit from it.

Now while these things were being said, and great shame was felt, certain holy men who had often succeeded in this kind of chase, and had thoroughly learned by experience that those who are armed with hope in God ought not to despair at all of such characters, kept a continual watch upon him, and if ever they saw him appear in the marketplace, they approached and saluted him. And at first he spoke to them from horseback, askance, as they followed by his side; so great was the shamelessness which had at first got possession of him. But they, being merciful and loving men, were not ashamed at all of this treatment, but continually looked to one thing only: how they might rescue the lamb from the wolves, which in fact they actually accomplished by means of their perseverance. For afterwards, as if he had been converted by some sudden stroke, and were put to shame by their great assiduity, if ever he saw them in the distance approaching, he would instantly dismount, and bending low would listen silently in that attitude to all which fell from their lips, and in time he displayed even greater reverence and respect towards them. And then, by the grace of God, having gradually rescued him out of all those entanglements, they handed him over again to his former state of seclusion and devout contemplation. And now he became so illustrious, that his former life seemed to be nothing in comparison with that which he lived after his fall. For being well aware by experience of the snare, and having expended all his wealth upon the needy, and released himself from all care of that kind, he cut off every pretext for an attack from those who wished to gain something from him; and now treading the path which leads to heaven, he has already arrived at the very goal of virtue. This man indeed fell and rose again while he was still young.

But another man, after enduring great toils during his sojourn in the deserts, with only a single companion, and leading an angelic life, and being now on the way to old age, afforded, I know not how, a little loophole to the evil one, through some satanic condition of mind, and carelessness; and although he had never seen a woman since he transferred himself to the monastic life, he fell into a passionate desire for intercourse with women. And first of all he besought his companion to supply him with meat and wine, and threatened if he did not receive it that he would go down into the marketplace. And this he said, not so much out of a longing for meat, as because he wished to find a means and pretext for returning into the city. The other being perplexed at these things, and fearing that if he hindered this he might drive him into some great evil, allowed him to have his fill of this craving. But when his companion perceived that this was a contemptible scheme, he openly threw off shame, and unmasked his pretense, and said that he must positively himself go down to the city, and as the other had not power to prevent him, he desisted at last from his efforts, and following him at a distance, watched to see what the meaning of this return could possibly be.

And having seen him enter a brothel, and knowing

that he had intercourse with a prostitute there, he waited until he had satiated that foul desire, and then, when he came out, he received him with uplifted hands, and having embraced and fervently kissed him, without uttering any rebuke on account of what had happened, he only besought him, seeing that he had satiated his desire, to return again to his dwelling in the wilderness. And the other, put to shame by his great clemency, was immediately smitten at the heart, and being full of guilt for the deed which he had perpetrated, followed him to the mountain and there he begged the man to shut him up in another hut, and, having closed the doors of the dwelling, to supply him with bread and water on certain days, and to inform those who inquired about him that he was laid to rest. And when he had said this, and persuaded him, he shut himself up, and was there continually, with fasting and prayers and tears, wiping off from his soul the defilement of his sin.

And not long after when a drought had settled on the neighboring region, and all in that country were lamenting over it, a certain man was commanded by a vision to depart and exhort this recluse to pray, and put an end to the drought. And when he had departed, taking companions with him, they found the man, who formerly dwelt with him, there alone; and on inquiring concerning the other they were informed that he was dead. But they, believing that they were deceived, betook themselves again to prayer, and again by means of the same vision heard the same things which they had heard before. And then, standing around the man who really had deceived them, they besought him to show the other to them, for they declared

that he was not dead but living. When he heard this, and
perceived that their compact was exposed, he brought
them to that holy man. And they, having broken through
the wall (for he had even blocked up the entrance) and all
of them having entered, prostrating themselves at his feet
and informing him of what had happened, besought him
to help them against the famine. But he at first resisted,
saying that he was far from such confidence as that, for he
continually had his sin before his eyes, as if it had only just
taken place. But when they related all which had happened
to them they then induced him to pray; and having prayed
he put an end to the drought.

**There is also the example of a disciple of St. John the
evangelist, who returned from a life of crime.**

And what happened to that young man who was at first
a disciple of John the son of Zebedee, but afterwards for
a long time became a robber chief, and then again having
been captured by the holy hands of the blessed apostle
returned from the robber dens and lairs to his former
virtue, you are not ignorant, but know it all as accurately
as I do. And I have often heard you admiring the great
condescension of the saint, and how he first of all kissed
the blood-stained hand of the young man, embracing him,
and so brought him back to his former condition.[2]

---

2   This story is told by Clement of Alexandria in his treatise, "Who is the rich
man that is saved?" and also provided by Eusebius in his *History of the Church*, 3.23.

Believe Repentance Is Beneficial

The apostle Paul mourned not over those who sinned, but rather over those who had not repented, as in the case of Onesimus the runaway thief, and those who sinned among the Corinthians.

Moreover also the blessed Paul not only welcomes Onesimus, the unprofitable runaway thief, because he was converted, but also asks his master to treat him who had repented on equal terms of honor with his teacher, thus saying: "I beseech you for my son Onesimus, whom I have begotten in my bonds, who was formerly unprofitable to you, but now is profitable to you and to me, whom I have sent back to you. Therefore, receive him, who is my very heart, whom I would gladly have kept with me, that on your behalf he might minister unto me in the bonds of the gospel; but without your consent I would do nothing, so that your goodness should not be out of necessity, but of free will. For perhaps he was therefore separated from you for a time, that you should have him back forever, no longer as a servant, but above a servant, a brother beloved, especially to me, but how much more to you, both in the flesh and in the Lord? If then you hold me as a partner, receive him as myself."[1] And the same apostle, in writing to the Corinthians, said, "Lest when I come I should mourn over many of those who have sinned beforehand and have not repented"; and again, "As I have said beforehand, so do I again declare beforehand, that if I come again I will not spare."[2]

Do you see who they are whom he mourns, and whom he does not spare?—not those who have sinned, but those who have not repented, and not simply those who have not repented, but those who have been called once and again to this work, and would not be persuaded. For the expression, "I have said beforehand and do now say beforehand, as if I were present the second time, and being absent I write," implies exactly that which we are afraid may take place now in our case. For although Paul is not present who then threatened the Corinthians, yet Christ is present, who was then speaking through his mouth; and if we continue obdurately, He will not spare us, but will smite us with a mighty blow, both in this world and the next.

---

1   Philemon 10–17
2   2 Corinthians 12:21; 13:2

**Accuse yourself first before someone else accuses you.
Let us make our Judge more merciful by our honesty
about what we are rightly accused of.**

Let us then anticipate His anger by our confession; let us
pour out our hearts before Him. For "you have sinned,"
we read, "do not add to that any more, and pray on behalf
of your former deeds";[3] and again, "a righteous man is his
own accuser in the first instance."[4] Let us not then linger
for the accuser, but let us seize his place beforehand, and
so let us make our Judge more merciful by means of our
candor.

**Do not confess your sins and yet have no hope in believing
you will gain by repentance. If you are convinced there
is no advantage of repentance, then it will be useless,
because it will be hard to sustain a life of righteousness
afterward. This hope is needed in order not to spoil the
fruit of repentance.**

Now I know indeed that you confess your sins, and call
yourself miserable above measure, but this is not the only
thing I wish, but I long for you to be persuaded that it
can justify you. For as long as you make this confession
unprofitable, even if you accuse yourself, you will not be
able to desist from the sins which follow it. For no one will

---

3   Sirach 21:1
4   Proverbs 18:17

be able to do anything with zeal and the proper method, unless he has first of all persuaded himself that he does it to advantage. For even the sower, after he has scattered his seed, unless he expects the harvest, will never reap. For who would choose to fatigue himself in vain, if he was not to gain any good from his labor? So then he also who sows words, and tears, and confession, unless he does this with a good hope, will not be able to desist from sinning, being still held down by the evil of despair; but just as that farmer who despairs of any crop of fruit will not in the future hinder any of those things which damage the seeds, so also he who sows his confession with tears, but does not expect any advantage for this, will not be able to overthrow those things which spoil repentance. And what does spoil repentance is being again entangled in the same evils. "For there is one," we read, "who builds, and one who pulls down; what have they gained more than toil? He who is dipped in water because of contact with a dead body, and then touches it again, what has he gained by his washing?"[5] Even so if a man fasts because of his sins, and goes his way again, and does the same things, who will listen to his prayer? And again we read "If a man goes back from righteousness to sin, the Lord will prepare him for the sword,"[6] and, "As a dog when he has returned to his vomit, and become repulsive, so is a fool who by his wickedness has returned to his sin."[7]

---

5   Sirach 34:23, 25
6   Sirach 26:28
7   Proverbs 26:11

End Well and You Will
Make It to Heaven

Being honest in declaring your sins is not good enough. Lots of people shamelessly do that. Being honest in declaring your sins and feeling shame is what is needed so your soul does not fall into more of the same sins.

Do not then merely set forth your sins, being your own accuser, but as one who ought to be justified by the method of repentance; for in this way you will be able to put your soul, which makes its confession, to shame, so that it falls no more into the same sins. For to accuse ourselves vehemently and call ourselves sinners is common, so to say, to unbelievers also. Many at least of those who belong to the stage, both men and women, who habitually practice the greatest shamelessness, call themselves miserable, but not with the proper aim. Wherefore I would not even call this confession, for the publication of their sins is not accompanied with compunction of soul, nor with bitter tears, nor with conversion of life, but in fact some of them make it in pursuit of a reputation for the hearers for candor of speech. For offenses do not seem so grievous when some other person announces them as when the perpetrator himself reports them. And they who under the influence of strong despair have lapsed into a state of insensibility, and treat the opinion of their fellowmen with contempt, proclaim their own evil deeds with much effrontery, as if they were the doings of others.

Laziness is the root of despair, and they both feed each other to keep you down. Break away from both in order to alleviate the depressing thoughts they give you.

But I do not wish you to be any of these, nor to be brought out of despair to confession, but with a good expectation, after cutting away the whole root of despair, to manifest zeal in the contrary direction. And what is the root and mother of this despair? It is laziness, or rather one would not call it the root only, but also the nurse and mother. For as in the case of wool, decay breeds moths, and is in turn increased by them, so here also laziness breeds despair, and is itself nourished in turn by despair; and thus supplying each other with this accursed exchange, they acquire no small additional power. If anyone then cuts one of these off, and hews it in pieces, he will easily be able to get the better of the remaining one. For on the one hand he who is not lazy will never fall into despair, and on the other he who is supported by good hopes, and does not despair of himself, will not be able to fall into laziness. Please then, wrench this pair apart, and break the yoke in pieces, by which I mean a variable and yet depressing habit of thought; for that which holds these two things together is not uniform, but manifold in shame and character.

Just because you did a lot of good things and then fell into just as much sin does not mean all the good you did will be forgotten. Rather, quickly turn your life around and do good, to overcome the weight of evil you have committed. Take advantage of your life here and now, shifting the balance so that your good deeds outweigh your evil ones. Even if at the end you are the not the brightest star, however, just like all stars, you will still find yourself shining in heaven.

And what is this? It happens that one who has repented has done many great and good deeds, but meanwhile he has committed some sin equivalent to those good deeds, and this especially is sufficient to plunge him into despair, as if the buildings which had been set up were all pulled down, and all the labor which he had bestowed upon them had been in vain and come to nothing. But this must be taken into account, and such reasoning must be repelled, because if we do not store up in good time a measure of good deeds equivalent to the sins which are committed after them, nothing can hinder us from sinking grievously and completely. But as it is, [right action] like some stout breastplate does not suffer the sharp and bitter dart to accomplish its work, but even if it is itself cut through, it averts much danger from the body. For he who departs to the other world with many deeds both good and bad, will have some alleviation in respect of the punishment and the torment there; but if a man is destitute of these good works, and takes only the evil with him, it is impossible to say what great sufferings he will undergo, when he is conducted to everlasting punishment. For a balance will be struck there between the evil deeds and those which are not such; and should the latter weigh down the scale they will to no small extent have saved the doer of them, and the injury arising from the doing of evil deeds is not so strong as to drag the man down from the foremost place; but if the evil deeds exceed, they carry him off into hell fire, because the number of his good actions is not so great as to be able to make a stand against this violent impulse.

And these things are not merely suggested by our own reasoning, but declared also by the divine oracles, for He Himself says, "He shall reward every man according to his works."[1] And not only in hell, but also in the kingdom one will find many differences, for He says, "In My Father's house are many mansions,"[2] and, "There is one glory of the

---

1   Matthew 16:27 (see also Romans 2:6)

2   John 14:2

sun, and another glory of the moon."[3] And what wonder, if in dealing with such great matters He has spoken with such precision, seeing that He declares there is a difference in that world even between one star and another?

Knowing then all these things let us never desist from doing good deeds, nor grow weary, nor, if we should be unable to reach the rank of the sun or of the moon, despise that of the stars. For if only we display that much virtue at least, we shall be able to have a place in heaven. And though we may not have become gold, or precious stone, yet if we only occupy the rank of silver we shall abide in the foundation; only let us not fall back again into that material which the fire readily devours, nor, when we are unable to accomplish great things, desist also from small ones, for this is the part of extreme folly, which I trust we may not experience.

> **God does not overlook the smallest of deeds to reward us for. It is not just the grand, good works that count, but also the little things we do, which we should not neglect, because God takes everything, small and big, into account, to compensate us in the afterlife.**

For just as material wealth increases if the lovers of it do not despise even the smallest gains, so is it also with the spiritual. For it is a strange thing that the Judge should not overlook the reward of even a cup of cold water, but

---

3   1 Corinthians 15:41

that we, if our achievements are not altogether great, should neglect the performance of little things. For he who does not despise the lesser things will exercise much zeal concerning the greatest; but he who overlooks the former will also abstain from the latter; and to prevent this taking place Christ has defined great rewards even for these small things. For what is easier than to visit the sick? Yet even this He responds to with a great recompense.

> End your life in a way that matches how you started it. Get off the ground, shake off the dust, and the devil will feel so defeated he will be less willing to come at you the same way again. And if we learn so much from other people's mistakes, consider how much more impactful it is when we learn from our own. Just do not despair, do not fall back. I will keep repeating this to you myself, and through others.

Lay hold then on eternal life, delight in the Lord, and supplicate Him; take up again the easy yoke, bow yourself beneath the light burden, put a finish to your life worthy of the beginning; do not allow so great a stream of wealth to slip past you. For if you should continue provoking God by your deeds, you will destroy yourself; but if before much damage has been done, and all your farming has been overwhelmed with a flood, you will dam up the channels of wickedness, you will be able to recover again what has been spoiled and to add to it not a little further produce.

Having considered all these things, shake off the dust,

get up from the ground, and you will be formidable to the adversary, for he himself indeed has overthrown you, as if you would never rise again; but if he sees you again lifting up your hands against him, he will receive such an unexpected blow that he will be less forward in trying to upset you again, and you yourself will be more secure against receiving any wound of that kind in the future. For if the calamities of others are sufficient to instruct us, much more those which we have ourselves undergone. And this is what I expect speedily to see in the case of your own dear self, and that by the grace of God you will have again become more radiant than before, displaying such great virtue as even to be a protector of others in the world above. Only do not despair, do not fall back, for I will not cease repeating this in every form of speech, and wherever I see you, as well as by the lips of others; and if you listen to this you will no longer need other remedies.

St. John Chrysostom's

SECOND
LETTER
TO
THEODORE

Do Not Be Discouraged
Falling Is Expected

I weep for you because you have erased your name from being counted among fellow Christians. I fear for you, because a person who is a Christian and then rejects their covenant with Christ will receive even greater condemnation than one who was not a Christian and fell.

If it were possible to express tears and groans by means of writing I would have filled the letter, which I now send to you, with them. Now I weep not because you are anxious concerning your patrimony, but because you have blotted out your name from the list of the brethren, because you have trampled upon the covenant which you had made with Christ. This is the reason why I shudder, this is the cause of my distress. On this account do I fear and tremble, knowing that the rejection of this covenant will bring great condemnation upon those who have enlisted for this noble warfare, and owing to indolence have deserted their proper rank.[1] And that the punishment for such is heavier than for others is manifest for this reason: no one would indict a private individual for shunning military service, but when once a man has become a soldier, if he is caught deserting the ranks, he runs a risk of suffering the most extreme penalty.

> There is nothing wrong with falling, but rather not getting back up. Even Christians who denied Christ because they could not stand the torture of persecution eventually returned to God and won the crown of martyrdom.

There is nothing strange, beloved Theodore, in a wrestler falling, but in his remaining in a fallen condition; neither is it a grievous thing for the warrior to be wounded, but to despair after the blow has been struck, and to neglect the wound. No merchant, having once suffered shipwreck, and lost his freight, desists from sailing, but again crosses

1   Consider here St. Paul's ominous words, as is written in his letter to the Hebrews: "Anyone who has rejected Moses' law dies without mercy on the testimony of two or three witnesses. Of how much worse punishment, do you suppose, will he be thought worthy who has trampled the Son of God underfoot, counted the blood of the covenant by which he was sanctified a common thing, and insulted the Spirit of grace?" (Hebrews 10:28–29). The Lord spoke of this covenant when He instituted the mystical supper: "For this is My blood of the new covenant, which is shed for many for the remission of sins" (Matthew 26:28).

the sea and the billows, and the broad ocean, and recovers his former wealth. We see athletes also who after many falls have gained the wreath of victory; and often, before now, a soldier who has once ran away has turned out a champion, and prevailed over the enemy. Many also of those who have denied Christ owing to the pressure of torture, have fought again, and departed at last with the crown of martyrdom upon their brows. But if each of these had despaired after the first blow, he would not have reaped the subsequent benefits.

Wounds from battle, physical or spiritual, do not give you reason to despair, because such wounds are normal and expected; therefore do not be disappointed with yourself as if you have been defeated entirely, but instead return bravely to finish the fight.

Even so now, beloved Theodore, because the enemy has shaken you a little from your position, do not then give yourself an additional thrust into the pit, but stand up bravely, and return speedily to the place from which you had departed, and do not deem this blow, lasting but for a little while, [as deserving] any reproach. For if you saw a soldier returning wounded from war you would not reproach him; for it is a reproach to cast away one's arms, and to hold aloof from the enemy, but as long as a man stands fighting, even if he is wounded and retreats for a short time, no one is so unfeeling or inexperienced in matters of war as to find any fault with him. Exemption from wounds is the lot of non-combatants, but those who advance with much spirit against the enemy may sometimes be wounded and fail, which is exactly what has now occurred in your case; for suddenly, while you attempted to destroy the serpent, you were bitten.

> **Do not be discouraged, but rather encouraged, because what happened to you was the evil one's response after seeing how committed you were to a life of goodness through devotion and spiritual exercises.**

But take courage, you need a little vigilance, and then not a trace of this wound will be left; or rather by the grace of God you will crush the head of the evil one himself; nor let it trouble you that you are soon impeded, even at the outset. For the eye, the keen eye of the evil one, perceived the excellence of your soul, and guessed from many tokens that a brave adversary would wax strong against him, for he expected that one who had promptly attacked him with such great vehemence would easily overcome him, if he persevered. Therefore he was diligent, and watchful, and mightily stirred up against you, or rather against his own head, if you will bravely stand your ground. For who did not marvel at your quick, sincere, and fervent change to good? For delicacy of food was disregarded, and costliness of raiment was despised, all manner of showiness was put down, and all the zeal for the wisdom of this world was suddenly transferred to the divine oracles; whole days were spent in reading, and whole nights in prayer; no mention was made of your family dignity, nor any thought taken of your wealth; but to clasp the knees and hasten to the feet of the brethren you did recognize as something nobler than high birth. These things irritated the evil one, these things stirred him up to more vehement strife; but yet he did not give a deadly blow. For if after a long time, and continual fasting, and sleeping on the bare ground, and the rest of the discipline, he overthrew you, even then there was no need to despair; nevertheless one would have said that the damage was great if defeat had taken place after many toils, and labor, and victories; but inasmuch as he upset you as soon as you had deprived yourself for the contest with him, all that he accomplished was to render you more eager to do battle with him. For that terribly evil pirate attacked you just as you were sailing out of the harbor, not when you had returned from your trading voyage, bringing a full cargo. And as when one has attempted to hold off a fierce lion, and has only grazed his skin, he has done him no injury but only stirred him up the more against himself, and rendered him more confident and difficult to capture afterwards; even so the common enemy of all has attempted to strike a deep blow, but has missed it, and consequently made his antagonist more vigilant and wary for the future.

Humanity: Easy to Fall, and to Recover

Human nature is frail, susceptible to falling, but likewise also can recover quickly. King David did some awful things, but afterward he recovered and was restored to his former position, and for his sake God bestowed blessings upon his son Solomon, despite Solomon's weaknesses.

For human nature is a slippery thing, quick to be cheated, but quick also to recover from deceit, and as it speedily falls, so also does it readily rise. For even that blessed man, I mean David the chosen king and prophet, after he had accomplished many good deeds, betrayed himself to be a man, for once he fell in love with a strange woman, nor did he stop there but he committed adultery on account of his passion, and he committed murder on account of his adultery; but he did not try to inflict a third blow upon himself because he had already received two such heavy ones, but immediately hastened to the physician, and applied the remedies: fasting, tears, lamentation, constant prayer, [and] frequent confession of the sin. And so by these means he propitiated God, insomuch that he was restored to his former position, insomuch that after adultery and murder the memory of the father was able to shield the idolatry of the son. For the son of this David, Solomon by name, was caught by the same snare as his father, and out of complaisance to women fell away from the God of his fathers.[1] You see how great an evil it is not to master pleasure, not to upset the ruling principle in nature, and for a man to be the slave of women? This same Solomon then, who was formerly righteous and wise but who ran a risk of being deprived of all the kingdom on account of his sin, God permitted to keep the sixth part of the government on account of the renown of his father.[2]

If what you had given up in despair was related to some worldly pursuits, I could have easily encouraged you by reminding you of your talents and persuaded you to return to what you had been doing and to work hard at it. But because what you despair of is related to the pursuit of heavenly things, I have to remind you of the judgment seat of Christ, who is now disregarded by you. He will

---

1   1 Kings 11:3, 4
2   1 Kings 11:12, 13

judge not just deeds, but thoughts too.

Now if your zeal had been concerned with worldly eloquence, and then you had given it up in despair, I should have reminded you of the law courts and the judgment seat and the victories achieved there and the former boldness of your speech, and should have exhorted you to return to your labors in that behalf. But inasmuch as our race is for heavenly things, and we take no account of the things which are on earth, I put you in remembrance of another court of justice, and of that fearful and tremendous seat of judgment: "For we must all be made manifest before the judgment seat of Christ."[3] And He will then sit as judge who is now disregarded by you. What shall we say then, let me ask, at that time? Or what defense shall we make, if we continue to disregard Him? What shall we say then? Shall we plead the anxieties of business? No, He has anticipated this by saying, "What shall it profit a man if he gain the whole world and lose his own soul?"[4] Or that we have been deceived by others? But it did not help Adam in his defense to screen himself behind his wife and say, "The woman whom You gave me, she deceived me,"[5] even as the serpent was no excuse for the woman. Terrible, O beloved Theodore, is that tribunal, one which needs no accusers and waits for no witnesses, for "all things are naked and

---

3   2 Corinthians 5:10

4   Matthew 16:26

5   Genesis 3:12

laid open to Him"[6] who judges us; and we must submit to give an account not of deeds only but also of thoughts, for that Judge is quick to discern the thoughts and intents of the heart.[7]

> Maybe you will give as an excuse your weak human nature, and that you couldn't bear the burden. That is no excuse at all, because what Christ is offering you is recovery from fatigue, and yet you find that too burdensome? What is more relieving than to be released from the troubles and worries of this life?

But perhaps you will allege weakness of nature as the excuse, and inability to bear the yoke. And what kind of defense is this, that you do not have strength to bear the easy yoke, that you are unable to carry the light burden? Is recovery from fatigue a grievous and oppressive thing? For it is to this that Christ calls us, saying, "Come unto Me all you that labor and are heavy laden, and I will give you rest; take My yoke upon you and learn from Me, for I am meek and lowly in heart; for My yoke is easy and My burden is light."[8] For what can be lighter, I ask, than to be released from anxieties, and business, and fears, and labors, and to stand outside the rough billows of life, and dwell in a tranquil haven?

---

6   Hebrews 4:13

7   Hebrews 4:12

8   Matthew 11:28–29

Christian Freedom Brings
Lasting Relief

**What do people in the world value the most? Wealth,
position, and reputation, you will say. Yet that is nothing
compared with the freedom Christians have. It is so easy
to lose all of those worldly things, but a Christian is never
subject to losing the loftiness of spiritual wealth, position,
and reputation due to some human interference, but only
if they succumb to the power of darkness.**

Which of all things in the world seems to you most
desirable and enviable? No doubt you will say government,
and wealth, and public reputation. And yet what is more
wretched than these things when they are compared with
the liberty of Christians. For the ruler is subjected to the

wrath of the populace and to the irrational impulses of the multitude, and to the fear of higher rulers, and to anxieties on behalf of those who are ruled, and the ruler of yesterday becomes a private citizen today; for this present life in no wise differs from a stage, but just as there, one man fills the position of a king, a second of a general, and a third of a soldier, but when evening has come on the king is no king, the ruler no ruler, and the general no general, even so also in that day each man will receive his due reward not according to the outward part which he has played but according to his works. Indeed glory is a precious thing which perishes like the power of grass, or wealth, the possessors of which are pronounced unhappy. "For woe," we read, "to the rich";[1] and again, "Woe unto them who trust in their strength and boast themselves in the multitude of their riches!"[2] But the Christian never becomes a private person after being a ruler, or a poor man after being rich, or without honor after being held in honor; but he abides rich even when he is poor, and is exalted when he strives to humble himself, and from the rule which he exercises no human being can depose him, but only one of those rulers who are under the power of this world's potentate of darkness.

"But there's nothing wrong with marriage," you'll say. I agree. However, after you have already been committed in marriage to the heavenly Bridegroom, deserting Him

---

1   Luke 6:24

2   Psalm 49:6

**for another is wrong, and in magnitude it is far worse
than adultery as much as God is greater than humans.**

"Marriage is right," you say; I also assent to this. For
"marriage," we read, "is honorable and the bed undefiled;
but fornicators and adulterers God will judge";[3] but it is
no longer possible for you to observe the right conditions
of marriage. For if he who has been attached to a heavenly
Bridegroom deserts Him, and joins himself to a wife, the
act is adultery, even if you call it marriage ten thousand
times over; or rather it is worse than adultery in proportion
as God is greater than man. Let no one deceive you saying,
"God has not forbidden to marry"; I know this as well as
you: He has not forbidden to marry, but He has forbidden
to commit adultery, which is what you are wishing to do.
And may you be preserved from ever engaging yourself in
marriage! And why do you marvel if marriage is judged
as if it were adultery, when God is disregarded? Slaughter
has brought about righteousness, and mercy has been a
cause of condemnation more than slaughter, because the
latter has been according to the mind of God but the
former has been forbidden. It was reckoned to Phinehas
for righteousness that he pierced to death the woman who
committed fornication, together with the fornicator;[4] but
Samuel, that saint of God, although he wept and mourned
and entreated for whole nights, could not rescue Saul
from the condemnation which God issued against him,

---

3   Hebrews 13:4

4   Numbers 25:7–11

because he saved, contrary to the design of God, the king of the alien tribes whom he ought to have slain.[5] If then mercy has been a cause of condemnation more than slaughter because God was disobeyed, what wonder is it if marriage condemns more than adultery when it involves the rejection of Christ? For, as I said at the beginning, if you were a private person no one would indict you for shunning to serve as a soldier; but now you are no longer your own master, being engaged in the service of so great a King. For if the wife has no power over her own body, but the husband,[6] much more they who live in Christ must be unable to have authority over their body. He who is now despised, the same will then be our Judge; think ever on Him and the river of fire, "For a river of fire," we read, "winds before His face,"[7] for it is impossible for one who has been delivered over by Him to the fire to expect any end of His punishment. But the unseemly pleasures of this life in no way differs from shadows and dreams, for before the deed of sin is completed, the conditions of pleasure are extinguished, and the punishments for these have no limit; and the sweetness lasts for a little while, but the pain is everlasting.

I know you are feeling quite weak now in the midst of your struggle with the evil one, but just reply back to him: "We do not serve you." Just turn your eyes upward, and

---

5   1 Samuel 15

6   1 Corinthians 7:4

7   Daniel 7:10

**while you are in the middle of the heat of the furnace of
fire, God will send you relief; just do not inwardly add to
the fire you are in, by what you tell yourself by your own
thoughts.**

Tell me, what is there stable in this world? Wealth, which
often does not last even to the evening? Or glory? Hear
what a certain righteous man says: "My life is swifter than
a runner."[8] For as they dash away before they stand still,
even so does this glory take to flight before it has fairly
reached us. Nothing is more precious than the soul, and
even they who have gone to the extremity of folly have
not been ignorant of this, for "there is no equivalent of
the soul" is the saying of a heathen poet.[9] I know that you
have become much weaker for the struggle with the evil
one; I know that you are standing in the very midst of the
flame of pleasures; but if you will say to the enemy, "We do
not serve your pleasures, and we do not bow down to the
root of all your evils," if you will bend your eye upward,
the Savior will even now shake out the fire, and will burn
up those who have flung you into it, and will send to you
in the midst of the furnace a cloud, dew, and a rustling
breeze, so that the fire may not lay hold of your thought or
your conscience.[10]

Only do not consume yourself with fire. For the
weapons and devices of besiegers have often been unable to
destroy the fortification of cities, but the treachery of one

---

8   Job 9:25

9   Homer's Iliad, Book 9, Line 401

10   Daniel 3, inclusive of the Prayer of Azariah, in accordance with the Septuagint.

or two of the citizens dwelling inside has betrayed them to the enemy without any trouble on his part. And now if none of your thoughts within betray you, should the evil one bring countless devices against you from without, he will bring them in vain.

Believe in Yourself, as Others Do

You have a lot of good people praying for you, believing you can recover, yet you yourself have seemingly given up. I beg you, do not do this great wrong to yourself.

You have by the grace of God many and great men who sympathize with your trouble, who encourage you to the fight, who tremble for your soul: Valerius the holy man of God, Florentius who is in every respect his brother, Porphyrius who is wise with the wisdom of Christ, and many others. These are daily mourning, and praying for you without ceasing; and they would have obtained what they asked for, long ago, if only you had been willing to withdraw yourself a little space out of the hands of the enemy. Now then is it not strange that, while others do not even now despair of your salvation, but are continually praying that they may have their member restored to them, you yourself, having once fallen, are unwilling to get up again, and remain prostrate, all but crying aloud to the enemy: "Slay me, smite me, spare not?" "Does he who falls not rise up again?"[1] speaks the divine oracle. But you are striving against this and contradicting it; for if one who has fallen despairs it is as much as to say that he who falls does not rise up again, I entreat you, do not do so great a wrong to yourself; do not pour upon us such a flood of sorrow.

> It's not because you are young—not even 20 yet—that I say this, because I would say the same thing even if you were very old: you are not justified in feeling despair. Think about examples such as the thief on the cross, and return to your former mindset I recall you saying often: "Do not delay in turning to the Lord."

I do not say at the present time, when you have not yet completed your twentieth year, but even if, after achieving many things, and spending your whole life in Christ you had, in extreme old age, experienced this attack, even then it would not have been right to despair, but to call to mind the robber who was justified on the cross, and the laborers who wrought about the eleventh hour, who received the wages of the whole day. But as it is not well that those who have fallen near the very extremity of life should abandon hope, if they be sober minded, so on the other hand it is

---

1   Jeremiah 8:4

not safe to feed upon this hope, and say, "Here for a while, I will enjoy the sweets of life, but afterwards, when I have worked for a short time, I will receive the wages of the whole working time." For I recollect hearing you often say, when many were exhorting you to frequent the schools:[2] "But what if I bring my life to a bad end in a short space of time, how shall I depart to Him who has said, 'Do not delay in turning to the Lord, nor put off day after day?'"[3] Recover this thought, and stand in fear of the thief, for by this name Christ calls our departure from here, because it comes upon us unawares.[4]

Life has so many anxieties that come upon us, and many in life work very hard, only to find themselves having died before they could enjoy all they labored for. [Do not let this happen to you.]

Consider the anxieties of life which befall us, both those which are personal to ourselves, and which are common to us with others: the fear of rulers, the envy of citizens, the danger which often hangs over us imperiling even life

---

2   Schools of pagan philosophy—maybe those over which Libanius presided in Antioch.

3   Sirach 5:7

4   Scripture often likens how unexpected death comes to us, catching us off guard, requiring us to suddenly be ready to give an account to the heavenly Judge, with the metaphor of a thief who unexpectedly at night breaks in to steal from us, against whom we must be ready to fend off or otherwise suffer loss. See Revelation 16:15, Matthew 24:43, and 1 Thessalonians 5:2, 4.

itself, the labors, the distresses, the servile flatteries (such as are unbecoming even to slaves if they be earnest-minded men), [and] the fruit of our labors coming to an end in this world, a fact which is the most distressing of all. It has been the lot indeed of many to miss the enjoyment of the things for which they have labored, and after having consumed the prime of their manhood in labors and perils, just when they hoped that they should receive their reward, they have departed, taking nothing with them. For if, after undergoing many dangers, and completing many campaigns, one will scarcely look upon an earthly king with confidence, how will anyone be able to behold the heavenly King, if he has lived and fought for another all his time.

PART

5

I Have Not Lost Hope in You

Think about the troubles and anxieties of this life when it comes to a wife and children. [Instead of focusing solely on serving God], do you prefer all of these other distractions instead?

Would you have me speak of the domestic cares of wife, and children and servant? It is an evil thing to wed a very poor wife, or a very rich one, for the former is injurious to the husband's means, the latter to his authority and independence. It is a grievous thing to have children, still more grievous not to have any; for in the latter case marriage has been to no purpose, in the former a bitter bondage has to be undergone. If a child is sick, it is the occasion of no small fear; if he dies an untimely death, there is inconsolable grief; and at every stage of growth there are various anxieties on their account, and many fears and toils. And what is one to say to the rascalities of domestic servants? Is this then life Theodore, when one's soul is distracted in so many directions, when a man has to serve so many, to live for so many, and never for himself?

> **Look at how carefree life can be, when your main focus, your only anxiety, is how you ought to please God?**

Now among us,[1] O friend, none of these things happen; I appeal to yourself as a witness. For during that short time when you were willing to lift your head above the waves of this world, you know what great cheerfulness and gladness you enjoyed. For there is no man free, except only he who lives for Christ. He stands superior to all troubles, and if he does not choose to injure himself no one else will be able to do this, but he is impregnable; he is not stung by the loss of wealth, for he has learned that we "brought nothing into this world, neither can we carry anything out."[2] He is not caught by the longings of ambition or glory, for he has learned that our citizenship is in heaven.[3] No one annoys him by abuse, or provokes him by blows. There is only one calamity for a Christian, which is disobedience to God; but all the other things, such as loss of property, exile, peril

---

1   St. John is referring here to the life of monasticism.

2   1 Timothy 6:7

3   Philippians 3:20

of life, he does not even reckon to be a grievance at all.
And that which all dread, departure from here to the other
world, this is to him sweeter than life itself. For as when one
has climbed to the top of a cliff and gazes on the sea and
those who are sailing upon it—he sees some being washed
by the waves, others running upon hidden rocks, some
hurrying in one direction, others being driven in another
like prisoners by the force of the gale, many actually in the
water, some of them using their hands only in the place of
a boat and a rudder, and many drifting along upon a single
plank, or some fragment of the vessel, others floating dead,
a scene of manifold and various disaster—even so he who
is engaged in the service of Christ, drawing himself out of
the turmoil and stormy billows of life, takes his seat upon
secure and lofty ground.

For what position can be loftier or more secure than
that in which a man has only one anxiety: "How he ought
to please God?"[4] Have you seen the shipwrecks, Theodore,
of those who sail upon this sea? Wherefore, I beseech you,
avoid the deep water, avoid the stormy billows, and seize
some lofty spot where it is not possible to be captured.
There is a resurrection, there is a judgment, there is a
terrible tribunal which awaits us when we have gone out of
this world: "We must all stand before the judgment seat of
Christ."[5] It is not in vain that we are threatened with hell
fire, it is not without purpose that such great blessings have
been prepared for us. The things of this life are a shadow,
and nothing more even than a shadow, being full of many

---

4   1 Thessalonians 4:1

5   Romans 14:10

fears, and many dangers, and extreme bondage. Do not then deprive yourself both of that world, and of this, when you may gain both, if you please. Now, that they who live in Christ will gain the things of this world, Paul teaches us when he says, "But I spare you,"[6] and again, "But this I say for your profit."[7] You see that even here he who cares for the things of the Lord is superior to the man who has married?

> The evil one puts you in despair by cutting off your hope. People have tried to convince me I should lose hope in your recovery too, but I did not listen to any of them, believing that, God willing, my letter will accomplish something. By God's grace, I trust that you will also do your part, and we shall again see you occupying an eminent place among the flock of Christ. Please reply to this letter, which will make us very happy.

It is not possible for one who has departed to the other world to repent; no athlete, when he has quitted the lists, and the spectators have dispersed, can contend again. Be always thinking of these things, and break in pieces the sharp sword of the evil one, by means of which he destroys many. And this is despair, which cuts off from hope those

---

6   1 Corinthians 7:28—"But even if you do marry, you have not sinned; and if a virgin marries, she has not sinned. Nevertheless such will have trouble in the flesh, but I would spare you."

7   1 Corinthians 7:35—"And this I say for your own profit, not that I may put a leash on you, but for what is proper, and that you may serve the Lord without distraction."

who have been overthrown. This is the strong weapon of the enemy, and the only way in which he holds down those who have been made captives is by binding them with this chain, which, if we choose, we shall speedily be able to break by the grace of God. I know that I have exceeded the due measure of a letter, but forgive me, for I am not willingly in this condition, but have been constrained by my love and sorrow, owing to which I forced myself to write this letter also,[8] although many would have prevented me. "Cease laboring in vain and sowing upon rock," many have been saying to me. But I listened to none of them. For there is hope, I said to myself, that God willing my letter will accomplish something; but if that which we pray against should take place, we shall at least have the advantage of escaping self reproach for keeping silence, and we shall not be worse than sailors on the sea, who, when they behold men of their own craft drifting on a plank, because their ship has been broken to pieces by the winds and waves, take down their sails, and cast anchor, and get into a boat and try to rescue the men, although strangers, known to them only in consequence of their calamity. But if the others were unwilling to be rescued no one would accuse those of their destruction who attempted to save them. This is what we offer, but we trust that by the grace of God you also will do your part, and we shall again see you occupying an eminent place in the flock of Christ. In answer to the prayers of the saints may we speedily receive you back, dear friend, sound in the true health. If you have

---

8   This evinces a previous letter, presumably what is referred to as St. John's first letter to Theodore.

any regard for us, and have not utterly cast us out of your memory, please vouchsafe a reply to our letter, for in so doing you will give us much pleasure.